AWAKEN THE Monster

7 Steps to Jumpstart your Sales Performance & Achieve Greater Success!

BY MICHAEL RAYMOND

Cover Illustration by Diana Deissler

For more information

Please Visit:

Awakenthemonster.com

MichaelRaymondSpeaks.com

Library of Congress Control Number:2012906627
CreateSpace, North Charleston, SC

This is book is dedicated to the Four Boys in my life:

Dean, Brad, Quinn and Kenny may it serve as an inspiration to you.

Never stop learning, Never stop improving, Never stop trying.

You are the person responsible for your own destiny.

Acknowledgments

To write a book has been a task that I have wanted to accomplish for quite some time. Several people have been instrumental to me throughout this process. The first is my amazing wife, Diane. Without her support and guidance I would not have even attempted such a task. She is an inspiration to me on a daily basis. My Mother and Father have been unwavering in their support of me, in good times and in bad. They have served as an example of a true partnership and I admire them both greatly.

Professionally, many people have been vital in providing me with the guidance needed to complete this book. Brian O'Connell's ability to transform my thoughts to words and for his commitment to this project. Big Bobby Sims, my Penn State Roommate, is a person who's knowledge into the sales process has been and continues to be so insightful. Joe Vassallo met me at one of the lowest points in my life and when few believed in me, Joe did. Lastly, Carl Fisher has been my constant support for countless years. His belief in me has been a great strength. Carl's own ability to rise up in the face of adversity has been a source of motivation to me.

Introduction

My name is Michael Raymond and I'm here to ask you for a few hours of your time—the time it takes you to read this book.

In exchange for that, I promise to change the way you look at your sales career and "jump-start" (yes, I chose that term for a reason) your passion for sales, for targeting a client and heading down that path to what you love to do best—close that deal.

I'm in sales, too, as a commercial cleaning business owner in the ultra-competitive, $94 billion US commercial cleaning industry.

Not many people give the cleaning industry a first thought, let alone a second one. But all across America, offices and commercial worksites are cleaned every night. It's a huge industry, with few barriers to entry. Make no mistake—selling this service requires skill, creativity, and tenacity—three key ingredients in success in sales.

Succeeding in that industry is all about making and establishing relationships, so people grow comfortable about giving you their business.

Succeeding in the cleaning sector is a tricky deal. After all, few people think about who cleans their offices or empties their trash.

But business owners and office building managers do—and there are enough of them out there that have made my business a big success. Sure, I had to establish relationships with all of them—and sell my name and reputation to every one of them, as well.

But you can learn a lot by putting your own neck on the line, and isn't that essentially what salespeople do every day? Making calls, chasing down leads, convincing hard-to-convince people that your product or service is so superior compared to your competition that it would be insane for your client not to reach for his or her proverbial checkbook.

Like I said, it's not easy, and after a while, it can wear a good sales professional down. After years of putting your neck on the line, the passion can wear thin, and the high success rate you've enjoyed over the years can lead to an alarming number of setbacks, even failures that we need to face (whether we want to or not).

It's a funny thing about setbacks. They are inevitable and we all experience them.

Henry Ford is actually a great example. He failed at just about every enterprise before he founded Ford Motor Company.

Or how about Fred Smith? While studying business management at Yale University, Smith nearly received a failing grade on a major business assignment. "The concept is interesting and well-formed," Smith was told, "but in order to earn better than a 'C,' the idea must be feasible."

Convinced of the viability of his proposal, however, Smith vowed to pursue it upon his return from the Vietnam War.

The idea? That parcels could be delivered overnight at a profit using a private airline system with a centralized hub. The resulting company? Federal Express.

Consequently, Smith survived his failed experience (but you have to wonder whether the Yale business professor did too.)

Smith is hardly alone:.

- In perfecting the incandescent lamp, Thomas Edison experienced ten thousand failures before he finally succeeded. A friend of Edison's remarked that ten thousand failures was a lot of failures, to which Edison replied; "I didn't fail ten thousand times. I successfully eliminated, ten thousand times, materials and combinations that wouldn't work."

- R. H. Macy failed seven times before his New York City department store caught on.

- British author J. K. Rowling suffered dozens of rejections from publishers before she sold her first Harry Potter book.

- Even Christopher Columbus had his setbacks. Originally, Columbus set out to discover a new trade route to India. He missed by half a globe. Yet who would call Columbus a failure?

I certainly would not. While I'm not as famous as the people mentioned above, I have experienced failure, too—and rebounded from it. I had a multimillion-dollar commercial services business that was my responsibility. Ultimately, it went under, and I with it.

But I learned from the experience and have come back to run yet another multimillion-dollar business.

That story—and others like it—is the backbone of the book you hold in your hands. You see, I believe that it is possible to jump-start your sales career and, as my book title shouts out, Awaken the Sales Monster that's inside of you.

....

"Success is not final, failure is not fatal: it is the courage to continue that counts."

—WINSTON CHURCHILL

....

Believe me, I've been there. When you're reeling from a downturn in your passion for sales, and quite likely a downturn in your sales numbers, the impact can be both devastating and humiliating. But as the anecdotes I've cited above attest, just about every figure in business that's known success has known failure too.

You don't have to take my word for it; just ask any Hollywood producer. Think of the last hit movie you saw. Chances are, the hero has certain consistent qualities in every culture: a common touch, a call to greatness, a critical trial, and a setback. Failure punctuates truly great leaders. They aren't great until they've failed. Failure is the crucible, the test. They deal with it, and their confidence and capabilities are enhanced.

The truth is, we need to fail. We need to fail to learn how to succeed. But our workplace culture certainly doesn't see it that way. We tend to turn our backs on failures—and failing individuals. But we do so at our own peril. After all, leadership comes from leveraging experiences taught by failure. In the business world, look at people like Jamie Dimon of JPMorgan Chase, who rose after being fired from Citigroup; and Jack Bogle, who founded Vanguard after being fired from Wellington Management.

Failure is liberating, and it is something you can use to guide future decisions. I believe the key is understanding not only where you failed, but why you failed—and then using that knowledge to guide future career decisions.

In this book, I'm going to show you how to revive your sales career, using some of the most effective business tenets in history. I'm going to show you how defeat energizes them to rejoin the fray with greater determination and vigor.

I'm also going to be brutally honest in this book. And I'm going to ask some uncomfortable questions. What prevents someone from rebounding from a sales career decline? Most salespeople who cannot recover have a tendency to blame themselves and are often tempted to dwell on the past rather than look to the future. They secretly hold themselves responsible for their career setback, whether they were to blame or not, and get caught in a psychological web of their own making, unable to move beyond the position they no longer hold.

Believe me, I don't want to minimize or trivialize the impact of a decline in passion for a sales career. I fully appreciate the difficulty of overcoming the debilitating psychological stress of failure, the challenges of failure to one's reputation (both personal and professional), social biases about failure, and other challenges which may be unique to one's company, its culture, and its industry. If not "tragic" or "devastating," a loss of passion almost always lowers one's self-esteem, is embarrassing, and has adverse financial consequences. More often than not, there is collateral damage to one's family members and/or to one's close colleagues at work, so guilt also comes into play.

Again, that happened to me. I lost my house, my marriage, and my business all within one year. I had launched my own building services business back in the 1990s. But I declared a personal bankruptcy and had a divorce in 1999. It seemed to happen so suddenly. One day I had a multimillion-dollar firm and a big house—all that fun stuff—and the next day, seemingly, lost it all.

But during the whole process, I never got down on myself. My buddies were telling me, "you should be on the edge of a bridge right now," but I never felt like that. I had already built a company up from nothing, so I knew I could do it again.

....

"I write to create something from nothing".

— HENRY DAVID THOREAU

....

Another big part of this book is to share the steps I took to shake off my bad experience. I'll be stressing the importance of doing what you know best (for me, that was the cleaning business).

I'll also be talking about rejuvenating your passion for life in general.

I learned that part of being divorced is losing 50 percent of your cash and 80 percent of your friends. So I had to build up my social network as well as my bank account—and I learned a lot in doing so.

Another key theme is to find out what you're good at—then excel at it. I took some time, examined my strengths and weaknesses, and ultimately founded a new janitorial business—and took the experiences I learned from the first business and applied it to my new business.

Why? Because I knew the cleaning business, and I was turning down a huge corporate job because I did not know what they wanted—but I did know janitorial business, up and down; I knew it cold.

I'll also be talking a lot about money, especially the importance of knowing your finances. In my case, I found that it's very easy to undervalue yourself—you have to know what you're worth.

Some other themes I'll be pounding away at in this book include the following:

Assess Your Situation: Job one in business and sales career regrowth is knowing where you stand at any given moment. After all, you can't map out a blueprint for success without having a starting point. I'll cover the key steps to take in assessing your current situation, i.e., stuck in a dead-end sales job, unemployed, running a failing small business, or switching careers.

Be Realistic: Blaming others for one's own problems in business is a tried-and-true blueprint for failure. I'll shed some light on the age-worn tendency to finger-point and blame and, instead, instruct you how to stop rationalizing and start actualizing a scenario where you can't help but succeed in sales.

What's Your Business Destination? Succeeding in sales is all about assessing your options, analyzing them, and acting on those options that give you the best chance for success—and for happiness. Some might call this goal setting, but more accurately, I call it figuring out your sales career "destiny."

Create a Winning Perception: In the sales game, who you are takes a backseat to how people perceive you. In this step, I'll describe how to set the right example in business, from knowing the ins and outs of business etiquette to dressing right to knowing how to give a presentation.

Crave Information: I will emphasize the importance of gaining information. Whether it's closing a sale or the reasons why you didn't get a sale, information is key. That means doing your homework, reading the right books, joining the right business networks, and becoming an expert in your own industry.

Brand Yourself for Sales Success: Personal branding is at the intersection of current business and societal trends. It enables you to profit from what separates you from other sales professionals with similar skills and abilities. I'll explain the myths and truths of personal branding and introduce readers to a customized three-step personal branding process. It has the power to turn you from "sales professional" to "sales monster."

Accentuate the Positive: Unearthing your unique promise of value by getting a clear picture of who you are and what you have to offer is a key step toward succeeding in sales. Virtually all top producers already have a personal brand that is defined by the perception of others. Yet many others cannot clearly articulate what their brands and goals are. The key is to focus on what you do well, and to do it better than anyone else—to the point where you "own" that task or responsibility.

Go the Extra Mile: There's an old saying that says, "no person who is enthusiastic about his work has anything to fear from life." In fact, the multibillionaire J. Paul Getty used to rank enthusiasm ahead of imagination, business acumen, and even ambition. In this chapter, I'll explain how enthusiasm, properly channeled, can help sales professionals to motivate themselves, do brilliant work, and actually always look to improve every day on the job.

Branch Out—and Don't Forget to Help Others: Like any successful person, you can benefit from having a well-nurtured professional network. I'll show you how to use that network to reach out and help others who need a lift up, just as I continually do.

Keep Your Eyes on the Prize: Achieving sales success is not a one-time effort. It's an ongoing career-management strategy. I'll include some tips and tools to keep your career continually moving in the right direction.

One more important theme:

Risk: It never goes away. Hey, I knew the drill. And I knew the risks. Start-up businesses have a very high failure rate in this country, with as many as 70 percent failing in their first two years. The reverse side of the coin is that many go on to prosper. I was pinning my hopes on becoming a member of the latter group, but that didn't happen—at least not right away.

But it did eventually happen: I did rebound and succeed in a new business venture—beyond my wildest dreams.

And you can, too.

What You Can Expect From This Book

Before I get into the nitty-gritty, I want you to know what to expect from me.

Structurally, this book will spell out, in step-by-step detail, how sales professionals can adopt winning themes and strategies and leverage them to achieve greater success in their careers—and their lives. I'd say the goal of the book is this: to pack every page with information on achieving success in sales using tried-and-true key steps, telling the story (I hope) in a clear, conversational, compelling way.

The book will also be full of useful graphics and sidebars (including my "Quality Tips—or "Q-Tips" in each chapter) revealing insights on some of the best-kept secrets in achieving sales success. Anecdotes and case studies from the front lines, from famous business and cultural figures, will also augment the text (i.e., "paint a picture"), to help readers visualize how others have tackled problems in trying to achieve success, and used those experiences to discover and harness their sales career passion.

I'll back everything up with easy-to-understand USA-Today-type info boxes, sidebars, and colorful industry profiles, and package it together in one lively, user-friendly book.

Ultimately, I want to tell you my story and the story of others who survived the same experience I did. My job here is to lay out a practical and user-friendly guide to rekindling your desire to sell like your life depended on it (and it might). Using these steps will help guide you through difficult circumstances, rebuild your confidence, and chart a new future.

I know that this journey of personal discovery is by no means easy. Nonetheless, it is one that must be initiated with commitment and then sustained by persistence throughout one's life. When setbacks occur—and they always do—the practical advice which I'll offer in this book will enable those who absorb and digest it to understand and (yes) accept what has happened, understand why it has happened, and then leverage that wisdom effectively and productively, not only in their sales careers but also in their personal lives.

As I began to write this book, I was reminded of Jack Dempsey's observation that "champions get up when others can't." Let's face it. All of us have encountered professional setbacks of one kind or another, and some of them are especially difficult to overcome.

My hope is that when you're done reading this book, you'll get up off the canvas and start swinging again—like you've never done before!

Let's cue the *Rocky* music and lace 'em up—and get "Jump-Started."

CHAPTER 1

Rise and Shine—Because Sales, Like Rust, Never Sleeps

....

Know where you stand and you'll never fall.

—ANONYMOUS

....

There's an old Chinese proverb that says failure either crushes a life, or solidifies it. The wounded oyster knows this—it mends its shell with pearls.

I like the imagery of that proverb. Taking a failure and recasting it with pearls is the whole idea behind the book you hold in your hands right now.

I know—it's a sensitive subject. Nobody in sales—where confidence is king—wants to talk about failure, or a bump on the road, let alone acknowledge it.

But history—particularly business history—is strewn with the carcasses of individuals whose careers failed, but who failed to learn from the experiences.

That's the problem.

Take the saga of "New Coke"—perhaps the poster child for business failure. In fact, if ever there were a failure destined to kill a career, New Coke was it. Sergio Zyman was the marketing man behind the most disastrous product launch since the Edsel. Wounded, he left Coca-Cola a year later and spent seven years consulting, invisibly. But Zyman bounced back into Coke, his ego intact and his title expanded.

How did he survive? It's a story worth telling. Zyman, then head of US marketing, was coming off his enormously successful introduction of Diet Coke when he was assigned day-to-day responsibility for top-secret Project Kansas in 1984. The zealous Mexican insisted that Coca-Cola (or Co-Cola, as he pronounces it) must act boldly to reverse its twenty-year market-share decline vs. Pepsi. Zyman, a former Pepsi marketer, argued that the correct strategy was to replace ninety-eight-year-old Coke with a better-tasting cola, label it "New Coke," and blare the news—which is exactly what the company did over a decade ago. Zyman's greatest error, which some attribute to ego, was that he and his team failed to present the option of keeping old Coke on the market.

But Coke not only survived—it thrived. The return of old-formula Coke 79 days after New Coke's launch produced the biggest-ever one-year rise in the brand's sales, reversed the share decline, and taught important lessons about the emotional bond of consumers to the product. The head of Coca-Cola was quoted as saying, "If I could have a New Coke situation every decade, I would. Absolutely."

Here are some other tales of business failure—and of redemption:

Graham Thomas Chipperfield, a star lion tamer with Ringling Bros. and Barnum & Bailey Circus, got back into the cage nine days after Sheba, one of his five-hundred-pound lionesses, mauled him. "It's always the trainer's fault," said Chipperfield. His doctors, who sewed eighty stitches into his back, advised him to rest for two months, but Chipperfield said, "I knew that if I stayed out, I would never get back in."

When Jan Leschly, the president of Squibb, was squeezed out after his company's 1989 merger with Bristol-Myers, he bid goodbye to corporate America for a year and took religion and philosophy courses at Princeton. But he never stopped focusing on his goal of being a CEO.

Set tangible goals, Leschly advises. In the 1960s, when he was among the world's top ten tennis players, the tall, stalwart Dane recalled, "My goal was not to be world champion. It was to play singles at Wimbledon Centre Court. So every time I practiced, I would imagine it, smell the grass, hear the crowds." In 1969, Leschly reached Centre Court (he was defeated by Rod Laver, Wimbledon's champ that year). He never lost sight of his goal. In 1994 he took the CEO's title at SmithKline Beecham.

Another rebounder is Robert Weber, a vice president in the residential lending division of the former First Union Mortgage in Wilmington, North Carolina. Weber's boss, Debra Warren, says she considered firing Weber in 1993, when First Union's volume exploded because of low mortgage rates. Weber, a broad-shouldered, likable fellow who had spent his career at First Union, dealt with the pressure of "refi mania," as it was called, by yelling, berating his staff, and making life hell for some of his three hundred employees. Working with Farr Associates, a Staub-Peterson competitor, Weber came to realize, "I'm the only person I can control. I've learned to be calm." His performance, measured by subordinates' written evaluations, improved, particularly in the areas of communication and listening. Said Warren: "For a while people were wondering, 'Is Bob sincere, or is he just acting differently to save his job?' He's won them over." You see, perception *can* become reality.

Mostly, the people involved in those failures simply quit—they were knocked to the mat and couldn't or wouldn't get back up on their feet. Hey, like I said in the introduction to this book, the sales business can wear even the best of us down. But you can't give up. The famed shipping tycoon Aristotle Onassis once said that you don't officially fail until you give up. In other words, giving up is not just quitting—it is actually choosing to fail.

Let me elaborate. If you're my age—a younger baby boomer—you might remember the Flying Wallenda's. They were a family that performed in circuses, mostly as a tightrope-walking act.

The father, Karl Wallenda, was a fabled tightrope walker, navigating canyons, bridge wires, and city buildings with characteristic calm and coolness. But eventually he was killed in a tragic fall.

His widow was quoted as saying, "All Karl thought about for three months straight months prior to the accident was failing—and to him, failing meant falling. It seemed to me that he lost faith, and put all his energy into not falling.

"Which is exactly what he wound up doing."

Of course, all setbacks aren't life ending, although it might seem like it at the time.

In the May 1, 1995, issue of *Forbes*, writer Brian Smith points out in his article *"So You Fail—Now Bounce Back!"* how some of the top names in US business have failed spectacularly—but lived to tell the tale.

> *History is littered with heroes who failed. An ad agency reportedly fired Walt Disney for a "singular lack of drawing ability," and Disney—not to mention Henry Ford—went bankrupt with early ventures before making money big-time. At General Electric, Jack Welch bombed early on. Tales of resurrection notwithstanding, most people view failure the way they do cancer—devastating, terminal, and too ugly to discuss.*

Q-Tip: **_Opening the Gates_**

Bill Gates, who regularly tempted failure at Microsoft, likes to hire people who have made mistakes. Said Gates, "It shows that they take risks. The way people deal with things that go wrong is an indicator of how they deal with change."

Reassessing after Sales Failure

I remember the film *The Gumball Rally*. In it, the Italian driver gets in the race car and removes the rearview mirror. "What's behind us," he said, "is not important."

When you're walking down the street, you're not looking back to see what you've passed, right? You're planning your next step so you can sidestep that lamppost or duck that low-hanging sign just around the corner.

Taking the next step in your sales career requires the same kind of planning. While it's true that starting a new business or switching careers is often a leap of faith, you first need to assess where you stand in order to plot the right course to achieve your goals.

In this chapter, I'll show you how to evaluate your situation, whether you're a laid-off sales professional looking to start a business from scratch, or you're jumping into a new industry, or you're recovering from a layoff and looking for a new sales gig. In any case you can name, the first step is to figure out what you already do well and what you need to improve upon in order to have success.

I know firsthand how difficult this first step can be, especially if you're moving on from a past failure or burned-out from selling the same product or service for years (even decades). And although we may think of planning as an exercise in logic and good sense, sometimes one of the most important parts of self-assessment is dealing with these emotions. Few of us have the benefit of moving from one success to another; for most of us, we reach a point in our sales lives where we need to move on in order to survive.

Let me give you an example. When I filed for bankruptcy, it could have been that point at which I said, "I can't go on." I could have given up. Instead, I didn't give up on myself, and I kept the faith that I could turn things around. This is an important realization: you need to forgive yourself and understand that failure is not something that is going to define you forever. As Winston Churchill once said, "Success is the ability to go from one failure to another with no loss of enthusiasm." What I've learned from personal experience is that there is great courage and pride that comes with being able to say you started at the very bottom before you climbed to the top. Every salesperson encounters failure at some point in his or her career, and it's a reflection of your character to be able to overcome it. They key is maintain a positive attitude.

Q-Tip: *The Change You Want Won't Happen by Accident*

To truly rejuvenate your sales, you have to go after it. Change isn't going to happen unless you make it happen. Thomas Jefferson observed about his own life, "The harder I work, the more luck I seem to have."

You too can have luck smile upon you by doing what Jefferson did his entire life—making his your own luck. Jefferson was born into a family where he had money and status. He could have just sat back and drifted along with few worries. Instead, he saw possibilities for a new nation that would give citizens more freedom than the nation had ever been known. He, like many of his contemporaries, wanted to turn that possibility into reality. He invested his time, money, and energy, willing to risk everything he had—including his life—in order to turn that possibility into actuality. And his willingness to invest all he had resulted in changing his future from one of a soft, lazy gentleman of means to one of the most important figures in history.

Like Jefferson, you must be willing to make the commitment and the short-term sacrifice to turn your possibilities into reality. Fortunately for us, we aren't risking our life, just our time, energy, and a bit of our resources. Nevertheless, turning our possibilities into reality can be just as life changing for us as fathering a new nation was for Jefferson.

Don't Point Fingers

Another component of your sales career recovery is refusing to blame others for your situation. Let's face it—when you're going through a tough time, it's easy to start separating yourself from everyone else as a kind of self-defense mechanism. Whether you're talking about coworkers, employees, or even a long-time customer, it makes failure just a little more palatable to tell yourself that it was their fault, not yours. Is this going to help you pick up the pieces and move on to success in your next endeavor? No, and in fact it could even hurt your chances by preventing you from looking objectively at what went wrong in the past. It's OK to examine the flaws of the people who were around you at the time, and you may even find that some of them probably shouldn't be involved in your next move. But resist the temptation to blame others for everything that went wrong.

I think what a lot of people neglect is how important our sales careers are to us. Yes, we all like to make a living, but we also define ourselves through our work. When someone loses a job or a business, that loss can take a real emotional toll. It's especially difficult these days, when you don't know if you'll get another chance in this tough economy we have. In many ways, losing a career is a lot like losing a loved one. You need to accept the fact that it's gone, and you need to get into the right mindset in order to move on. The same is true of someone who is instead perhaps stuck in a dead-end sales job they no longer enjoy. Those people, too, can feel as though they'll never get the chance to try something new, to take that leap of faith. Well, as I'll show you throughout this chapter, moving on is all about overcoming your fears and anxieties and taking a realistic, measured approach to setting yourself up for success.

So let's get started: for any of the reasons mentioned above, you are at an important turning point in your career. You want to start fresh, and you're ready to take a good hard look at where you are in relation to where you want to be. But where do you go from here?

Q-Tip: *Be an Optimist*

Denial, up to a point, is not a bad thing. Martin Seligman, a professor of psychology at the University of Pennsylvania, has done what he calls optimism studies of employees in thirty industries. Says he, "The people who bounce back are optimists who believe 'My problem is temporary, related to the particular situation I'm in, and not my fault.' Pessimists, who generally don't come back, see their failure as permanent, pervasive, their fault."

Retrace Your Steps

The first step in knowing where you stand is to retrace your steps to figure out how you got there. As I said earlier, do not mistake this process for playing the blame game—your objective is to rationally and objectively look at the decisions you made and the circumstances that led you to this point. You'll likely find that you made some mistakes—probably lots of them. You may also discover that many factors were beyond your control. The most important thing to take away from this is to learn from your failures. One of the worst things you can do in this situation is to jump right into another opportunity without performing this self-assessment (as well as a little bit of soul-searching), because you'll end up repeating the same mistakes all over again.

Another important step in figuring out where you stand is to look around you to get your bearings. In my case, I looked at other people in the cleaning industry—I tried to see who was having success, who wasn't, and why that was. Nobody ever does business in a vacuum, and a lot of the problems that plagued your past efforts are probably the same ones plaguing other people in your industry. This is a great time to read up on the people in the sales business who have made it to the top. Figure out what they did right and lay out what you'll have to do in order to make the same kind of moves.

Once you've come to terms with your current standing, the fun part begins. There are several areas of this you'll need to cover, so let's go through them, one by one, and get you going on the right track.

Planning ahead: OK, so you've established that things went wrong in the past, or not as well as you would have liked. What happens now? You can't reach the top floor if you don't know where the elevator is, and starting out you'll need to identify the most basic components of your new plan in order to get anywhere. Do you want to stay in the same industry? Do you want to be in the same location? Which people will you want to work with? Plot out your course, leaving nothing to chance—don't just assume that you'll fill in the holes later. In the cleaning business, for instance, the job is only done once you've swept and scrubbed everything—you can't just say, "Oh, I'll empty out this trash can later." Figure out what steps you'll need to take to get to where you want to be.

This can be a difficult process for some, especially if they're suddenly figuring out that they're very far down the ladder. Well, that's what planning ahead is all about—you need to face the facts and figure out if your dreams are worth some sacrifices. But don't assume that people achieve success through shortcuts. You need to put in the time and effort. If you need additional education, get it; if you're starting out in a new industry, take a part-time job or apprenticeship in the business. Remember, you could be restarting at the ground floor now, but you won't be for long if you're making up your mind to move forward.

Finding your sales passion: Sure, you want to make money—doesn't everybody? The question you really need to ask yourself is what will it take to make you excited to go into work each day? In my case, I was passionate about the cleaning industry. One of my friends was really into riding bikes, on the other hand. It started out as a hobby for him, but gradually he moved from riding bikes, to fixing them, to selling them, to finally manufacturing them. Now his passion is his career.

This is an especially important lesson for those who are coming out of a dead-end sales job or business startup. In many cases, that person may find, reflecting back on it, that a particular endeavor failed because he or she simply lost interest in it. On the flip side, it's always easier to be successful at a career that energizes you and inspires you to keep taking the next step. Will passion result in profit? Not always, but it will help weather those difficult early goings when the only reward is a day's work completed.

Assessing your abilities: What are you good at? Meeting prospects? Negotiating? Closing deals? Don't mistake past failures for reflections of your abilities. Many times people will look at a failed business venture or a layoff as an indication of their own lack of skills. But you'd be doing a disservice to your-self—and your future career—if you discounted all of your strengths that have carried you to this point.

Establishing your network: No matter where you're coming from, there were at least a few people involved in your last sales position who were working either for you or with you. And while many people find that a failed business or layoff eliminates many of these people from their lives, the truth is that they need to maintain these contacts that will help them get going again in their next venture.

This is the point at which you need to start being objective about which peo-ple are going to be valuable toward that end. Who has contacts in the industry you want to work in? Who is going to be a valuable business partner or employee for you? If you're starting a job search, for instance, it's vital to your own chances for landing a position to start organizing your network and letting people know about your situation. Nobody achieves success on their own; you need others— whether they're good friends or distant business contacts—to give you a hand along the way.

Assessing your needs: If you've been bitten once in the past, you're going to be much more cautious the next time you start a new business or relaunch a new sales career. And part of overcoming that fear is determining your toler-ance for risk and sacrifice. Of course, every leap of faith is going to require some courage. But if you figure out ahead of time what you're willing to undertake to achieve your goals, you'll ensure that your time will be spent wisely.

Keep in mind that every new beginning is going to lead to some sacrifice. If success were easy, you wouldn't have had any troubles the first time, right? After all, everybody would have already achieved it. Be realistic, but also identify the key factors that will come into play—things like your financial situation, your geographic location, your family obligations, and so on. If you discover that the hot new career you've imagined requires an education beyond your means, plan on making some changes in your life to get the skills you need anyway—take night courses, for example, or volunteer in that industry to pick up some skills and contacts.

The last thing you want to do is start your new career path and then realize halfway in that you weren't prepared to make some of the sacrifices that job or business demands. Know ahead of time what you're willing to give.

If you follow these instructions, hopefully you'll find that your next career stop in sales isn't as far away as you first imagined. In fact, one of the best ways to jump-start your sales career is to start this process right away—don't let your doubts and fears cloud your vision. You already know you have what it takes to go after success, or else you wouldn't have tried that the first time.

Sometimes when we go through tough times, we tend to see things as much worse than they really are. As I've mentioned, almost everybody suffers defeat at some point. The most important thing you can do after these situations is to pick yourself up, dust yourself off, and figure out what your next move is going to be.

In the next chapter, I'll talk more about taking responsibility for yourself and your past mistakes. You'll find that even though it's not fun to look at what could have been, the process will help you become a better and smarter person in your next career.

Q-Tip: *Stay Positive*

Jimmy Johnson, the legendary former coach of the Dallas Cowboys, says, "I was always emphatic that we wouldn't accept anything but being in the Super Bowl." He knows defeat. In 1989, his first season in Dallas, Johnson's record was 1-15, only a shade less humiliating than his career-launching 0-10 performance in 1966 as defensive coach of the Picayune High School Maroon Tide in Mississippi. Says Johnson, "At times people looked at me like I was a crazy man because we had the worst team in the NFL. But I never wavered in my attitude."

The Cowboys, of course, won the Super Bowl. Twice. Johnson, who has a college degree in industrial psychology, believes the turnaround hinged largely on positive thinking. Instead of telling a running back, "Don't fumble," he would say, "Protect the ball." He'd instruct a place kicker, "Make this," never, "Don't miss." Johnson says that his post-game meetings in Dallas were quick ones, concentrated on plotting the next win, "so we could put a loss behind us quickly."

Add Some Attitude to Your Sales Destiny

We'll spend a lot of time in this book discussing the key attributes career professionals must display to get ahead in the workplace. One of those attributes, I believe, takes precedence over any other, and that is *attitude*—specifically, a positive "can-do" attitude.

History abounds with tales of experts who were convinced that the dreams of others could never come to fruition. However, accomplishment came to those who said, "I can make it happen."

Take the Italian sculptor Agostino d'Antonio, who worked diligently on a large piece of marble. Unable to produce his desired masterpiece, he lamented, "I can do nothing with it." Other sculptors also worked this difficult piece of marble, but to no avail. Michelangelo discovered the stone and visualized the possibilities in it. His "I can make it happen" attitude resulted in one of the world's masterpieces—*David*.

Even the great Thomas Alva Edison discouraged his friend Henry Ford from pursuing his fledgling idea of a motorized car. Convinced of the worthlessness of the idea, Edison invited Ford to come and work for him. Ford remained committed and tirelessly pursued his dream. Although his first attempt resulted in a vehicle without reverse gear, Henry Ford knew he could make it happen. And, of course, he did.

There are other, more humanistic ways to separate "can-do" sales visionaries from the rest of the pack. Real sales visionaries seem to know who they are and how to relate to others. They know how to relate to clients and they know how to communicate with everyone inside the workplace, from the intern in the mailroom to the company president.

In addition, sales visionaries take career setbacks in stride. They know how to find something positive in every negative experience. Rather than feeling victimized over the fact that they didn't close a deal, they focus on what they can learn from the situation. They may find that they need to brush up on their presentation skills or polish up their industry knowledge. In this way, even their disappointments become a stepping-stone, not a roadblock.

"The Vision Thing"

So what strategies work best for the positive-thinking sales professional?

I've got a list of strategies—it's not a long one—of tactics I use to keep my sales skills sharp. As I've said, adopting a "winners expect to win" mindset is at the top of that list.

But not far behind is having a vision for success in my sales efforts. Or, as former President George Bush Sr. memorably called it, the "vision thing."

How do you define vision from a sales point of view? For my money, vision is a mental picture of your desired future state. Your vision represents what you are working for—not just money and business goals but personal goals as well.

Make no mistake, your clients have a vision, too—and it should help shape your vision. A client will tell you what their world looks like and how it operates, and explain all their current and future needs. This data allows you, the sales professional, to customize a solution.

But too many sales professionals don't get the "vision" thing. At the business seminars I attend, I meet a lot of people in sales. When I talk to them about having a vision, they tend to shrug their shoulders and tell me that "vision" is something a CEO or business owner needs to worry about—not them. But every sales professional should have a vision—a target for where they're headed in their careers. One of my business associates has a vision of being a soccer coach for his son's team—that's his vision, his target. I told him that he could "hit" that target if he worked harder in the winter, when soccer was out of season. Then when spring came, he'd be ahead of the game and would have more time to coach his son's team, without hurting his career.

I told my colleague that he had to visualize working harder to reach his target—then do it. That's what vision can do for you—it gives you a sense of direction and purpose, enabling you to allocate your own resources well, to develop and grow. For sales professionals, vision unites all the disparate elements of their careers—such as contact development, relationships and closing—and helps to formulate an overall strategy. It implies continuity—a future for both the sales professionals and his or her client that, if communicated effectively, gives the sales professional clear goals. This encourages effort and achievement.

In my view, vision is all about setting direction—you know, setting targeted goals (something I'll talk about in greater detail more specifically later in this book). In my own story, I found that the function of rebounding from a sales setback—like the loss of a client—is to produce change; setting the direction of that change is fundamental to success. Setting direction is never the same as planning, although people often confuse the two. Planning is an arduous process, deductive in nature and designed to produce orderly results, not change. Setting a direction is more inductive. Individuals must gather a broad range of data and look for patterns, relationships, and linkages that help explain things. What's more, the direction-setting aspect of taking charge of your sales career does not produce plans; it creates vision and strategies.

As I said, those are some of the key themes I'll be discussing throughout this book—all wrapped up in a cool new sales rejuvenation system that works for everyone—no matter what you sell or what industry you work in.

With the above thoughts in mind, let's kick it up a notch in Chapter Two.

Q-Tip: *Mmm, Mmm Good: A Cleaning Story*

Years ago, when I was working for a commercial cleaning business, I landed a major client—Campbell Soup. But in taking the job on, I learned a valuable lesson.

I was talking with the chief executive officer one day and he pointed out something that my crew and I had overlooked: after his office was clean, he noted that the dimples in the carpet from the imprint of his chair weren't in the same place. Ever the perfectionist, the CEO wanted the imprints to be in the same exact place every morning when he walked into his office.

As odd as I thought it was at the time, it was a great little lesson that every sales professional can learn from: attention to detail, structure, planning, thoroughness on the job, and good customer satisfaction. That's what is important, to look at the smallest detail through your customer's eyes.

Case Study: Building Something Big at Home Depot

When Bernie Marcus was growing up in New Jersey, he wanted to become a doctor. Instead he became a pharmacist after graduating from Rutgers University. The job didn't last long—within a few years he moved to retail sales. Marcus steadily climbed the corporate ladder, eventually becoming an executive with Los Angeles-based Handy Dan Home Improvement Centers. There he met Arthur Blank, Handy Dan's chief financial officer. Though both men thought their standing was secure at the company, Marcus and Blank were abruptly fired.

But the pair left Handy Dan with more than just the shirts on their backs. While working for the retailer, Marcus and Blank had explored the now ubiquitous sales technique known as discounting. They noticed that the more something was marked down, the more people there were who would buy it, which in turn increased volume and cut buying costs for the company. What if that theory could be put to the test through a large chain of warehouse-sized home improvement stores that bought and sold for cheap?

That idea might have gotten some laughs at that time in the late '70s, but Marcus, then unemployed, saw an opportunity. He and

Blank, along with business partner Ken Langone, who had encouraged Marcus to pursue the idea and provided the financial backing, opened their first Home Depot stores in Atlanta in 1979. Over thirty years later, there are now more than two thousand of them around the world—not bad for two guys who couldn't even cut it with Handy Dan.

When you've got a clean slate in front of you, you want to get off to a good start. Here are a few "dos" and "don'ts" as you assess your next career move:

Do This	Not That
Do take time to collect yourself after a sales failure or setback. Take time to see where things went wrong and how you could avoid those problems next time.	*Don't play the blame game. Neither you or those involved in your past career deserve the blame for everything that went wrong, and dwelling on this thinking will only prevent you from looking at your situation objectively.*
Do look around the industry you want to "sell"—what are the successful people doing? What's tripping up the others? Read books, go online, and find out as much as you can.	*Don't start a new sales career direction without a plan. Know where you'll start out, what you'll have to do to climb the ladder, and what your goals will be. Don't leave things to chance.*
Do go through your network and start contacting people who might be able to help you out in your new sales life. Identify the people and businesses that were successful for you in your past endeavor.	*Don't jump into an entirely new field if you have skills better suited for the industry you were just in. Sometimes all it takes are a few tweaks and a smarter approach to make your next venture successful.*
Do maintain an optimistic outlook.	*Don't let the past get you down; take pride in the fact that you now have a chance to build your next success from the ground up.*

Chapter Summary

· ·

Here are the keys to turning a potentially career-busting sales failure into future success:

- **Seek out a crisis**. Sometimes taking responsibility for a big mistake can help you stand out in the corporate crowd.

- **Visualize the next big win**. You can't let setbacks keep you from focusing on the ultimate goals.

- **See yourself as others do**. Another perspective on yourself, no matter how humiliating, can open your eyes to what you can best achieve.

CHAPTER 2

What Babe Ruth
Can Teach You About Sales

I'm in sales, just like you, and if there's one thing I want you to take away from this book, it's this:

To beat sales career fatigue, stay positive, and you'll stay profitable.

Take Babe Ruth (I'm a Phillies fan, but I don't mind using a Hall-of-Famer—even a Yankee—to make a point).

The Babe had a great attitude and it paid off, production-wise. Think about it. How many home runs did Babe Ruth hit? 714.

How many times did he strike out? 1,330.

Do people care about how many home runs he hit? Did he get paid for it? Did he get recognition and satisfaction?

Do people care about how many times he struck out? Why not?

When he struck out, he talked to himself in a positive way. He kept the bat in his hands.

He respected the competition. He loved where he played. He supported his boss and teammates. He kept himself in the ballgame mentally so he was always in a position to do what he did best.

What the Babe was doing was what sales professionals who are battling career burnout should be doing every day—practicing attitude control. And applying the formidable power of affirmations.

I understand that's not easy. I've owned and lost enough companies to know that. The sales gig can totally wear you down and there's not always enough room for positive energy. Or any kind of energy, for that matter.

You know what they say—adversity is the grindstone of life.

It's a great line, and one I can definitely relate to.

My take? Intended to polish you up, adversity also has the ability to grind you down. I saw that in my own experience running my own business—one that ultimately didn't work out, as I explained earlier in this book. I discovered, while fighting my way back from my own financial and career troubles, that the impact and ultimate result of these admittedly negative experiences depend on what you do with the difficulties that come your way.

I'm hardly alone. American stage director Eugene Hare hit the nail right on the head when he said, "Life is a game of cards. The cards are shuffled and the hands are dealt. You must play your cards well."

So it goes in the sales world, where the stakes are high and the expectations to succeed even higher. No, I'm not advocating you treating your sales career like a high-stakes poker game. But there are ways to get ahead in sales that exceed anything you'll win at a Vegas blackjack table.

To me, the biggest key in playing the hand you've been dealt is to refuse to lose. Let me clarify. Once you've experienced a setback, i.e. you've lost a client, blew a sale, or didn't hit your monthly mark, your confidence is going to take a hit—there's no doubt about that.

It's how fast you put that negative experience behind you that will set the stage for your future success—in other words, how long will it take you to stop looking backward and start looking forward?

Consider the phenomenal achievements of people experiencing adversity—and bouncing back from it. These guys weren't in sales, but the lessons they provide to us should be embraced by the rest of us who are in sales.

- Beethoven composed his greatest works after becoming deaf.

- Sir Walter Raleigh wrote the *History of the World* during a thirteen-year imprisonment.

- If Columbus had turned back, no one could have blamed him, considering the constant adversity he endured. Of course, no one would have remembered him either.

- Abraham Lincoln achieved greatness by his display of wisdom and character during the devastation of the Civil War.

- Luther translated the Bible while enduring confinement in the Castle of Wartburg.

- Under a sentence of death and during twenty years in exile, Dante wrote the *Divine Comedy*.

- John Bunyan wrote *Pilgrim's Progress* in a Bedford jail.

What is the one character trait that each of these individuals shares with one another? I'd say it's an inner resolve that tells people "winners expect to win". When I go out on a job, I expect to get it, just like Michael Phelps expects to win every swim race he enters. It is said that all that is necessary to overcome adversity is this: act as if it were impossible to fail.

That's a great mantra for people searching for answers after a sales disaster: failure is not an option.

Q-Tip: *Keep a Positive Attitude, Part II*

Words to live by for salespeople looking to jump-start their careers:

The longer I live, the more I realize the impact of attitude on life. Attitude, to me, is more important than facts. It is more important than the past, than education, than money, than circumstances, than failures, than successes, than what other people say or do. It is more important than appearance, giftedness, or skill. It will make or break a company...a church...a home.

The remarkable thing is we have a choice every day regarding the attitude we will embrace for the day. We cannot change the inevitable. The only thing we can do is play on the one strength we have, and that is our attitude. I am convinced that life is 10 percent what happens to me and 90 percent how I react. And so it is with you...we are in charge of our attitudes. — Charles Swindoll.

Sales Career Rejuvenation Action Steps

Yes, I advocate a positive attitude to wrestle burnout to the ground. But are there more concrete action steps you can take to fight career burnout and get back to your career mojo?

The short answer is "yes." As I've found out, it's not easy, but it's doable. I've learned—sometimes the hard way—that succeeding in sales isn't really all that complicated.

It's all about assessing your options, analyzing them, and acting on those options that give you the best chance for success—and for happiness. Some might call this goal setting, but more accurately, I call it figuring out your sales career "destiny."

One of my favorite salesmen of all time, Chrysler CEO Lee Iacocca, says meeting your sales destiny is the "the ability to concentrate, and to use your time well. This is is everything if you want to succeed in business—or almost anywhere else for that matter."

Or, as that other fabled philosopher Yogi Berra put it, "If you don't know where you're going, you'll end up somewhere else."

My take? Meeting your own sales destiny simply means defining where you're going. Actually, it reminds me of the process writing this very book—at a hundred and fifty pages or so, that destination looks like a daunting task.

But if you break it down chapter-by-chapter, page-by-page, and line-by-line—then it's actually manageable. It's the same if you're on a diet and you're aiming to lose twenty pounds—taking it one pound at a time is the way to go. Taking the issue one bite at a time, as it were, makes completing your voyage and meeting your destination much easier to handle.

So Rule #1 is this: don't set broad goals, set incremental ones. When Julius Caesar developed the calendar we use today, he had no idea that he was setting the stage for so many broken New Year's resolutions. But New Year's resolutions don't work because they're broad goals, and not specific ones. Same thing in sales.

Let me give you an example. I knew a guy who owned a lot of commercial office properties. I wanted the contract to clean those properties. I sent brochures, I called him on the phone—basically I did everything I could to land that account. Finally, I simply asked him if I could come in to his office and talk to him about what he was looking for a in a cleaning company.

I went to the meeting, listened to the guy, and went out and spent the next six months doing everything he told me to do. Then I came back and told him I knew exactly what he wanted and that I could deliver it for him.

He gave me the job on the spot. That's what I mean about "specific" goals—in this case, making sure to listen to clients and find out what they expect.

The way I look at goal setting and finding your destination is this: change the way you sell. These days, people and business are looking for value. That's why money is tight and customers are throwing nickels around like manhole covers. So you have to be adaptable—in tough environments, it's time to sell based strictly on value and cost.

Q-Tip: *Is Fatigue Killing Your Sales Career?*
The number one challenge—going away—in overcoming adversity and succeeding in sales again is burnout. Growing tired of the

same old, same old presents a myriad problems, but one of the most common is how it affects your own sales presentation skills.

Think about it. Have you heard your own sales pitch lately? And if so, does it strike you as dated and stale?

Let's face it, if we've grown tired of hearing ourselves talk, imagine how our clients feel.

My experience is that the more downtrodden we become with our own message, the less receptive a prospect will be. In addition, when we observe the resultant fatigued look on the prospect's face, we conclude our sales approach must be unappealing.

The result? Your incentive to sell deteriorates, and your sales will likely decline, too.

How to wake up and smell the sales? Try these tips:

1. **Slow down**. I know you've heard your own sales presentation a million times, but the prospects haven't. Give them the opportunity to absorb and process the valuable information you are sharing.

2. **There is no such thing as a generic prospect**. After you've called on a few hundred prospects, they can all look the same. When you see them in this light, they can tell. Just remember how important your favorite teachers made you feel when they treated you as an individual. People you make feel important frequently do one thing—buy from you.

3. **It's in the eyes**. If you're in front of a prospect, you must make constant eye contact. It will greatly enhance communication quality and will let you know what he or she is thinking. Let his or her eyes guide your presentation.

4. **Listen.** The questions prospects ask are everything. These questions will tell us everything we need to know in order to sell them. Giving prospects all the room they need to speak will move mountains when

it comes to revitalizing how your prospects and you perceive your presentation.

Q-Tip: *Salesperson, Heal Thyself*
To get a better sense of how clients perceive you, tape-record a random sampling of your phone calls to potential customers. Listen to the tape and assess your tone and voice. How did you sound? Would you want to speak with a person who sounds like you? What about your words? Were they clear and benefits-oriented? Taping gives you the opportunity to self-correct your presentation.

Bouncing Back: How to Become a "Sales Visionary"

One of the big things weary salespeople forget is how to listen to customers— then learning to give them what they want.

That's a big advantage when you're trying to get your sales career back on track. Most sales professionals don't listen to their customers, so when you do, it's a big benefit.

Relearning that ability is key to revitalizing your sales career. I firmly believe that. Sometimes we get so jaded in sales that we forget the bread-and-butter strategies that launched our careers in sales in the first place.

When sales are robust and things are going well, there is no reason to recreate the wheel. But when things go wrong, when you feel the walls collapsing around you, it's time to get back to basics and hit the reset switch.

That's like an old friend of mine (I'll call him "Sam"—I don't want to embarrass him), who hadn't been happy at his job for several years, even though he was meeting his quotas and appeared, on the surface, at least, to be doing OK.

But Sam didn't have a handle on what was wrong, and what he needed to do to re-engage his career and wake himself up in the process. I know from personal experience that when you're trying to make a big shift from where you are to where you want to be, small, incremental moves often won't be enough. Just like the fire marshals out in the wilderness that trigger "controlled" fires to keep forests alive and healthy, sometimes making a bold, dramatic move is the best option for resetting your career path.

But you don't want to venture out recklessly, especially if you have financial obligations and others depending on you. So, here's what you can do to start defining your sales career while keeping one foot planted in your current reality.

- *Visualize what you want.* It's easy to define what we don't want, but much harder to articulate what we *do* want. For example, it's more common to find ourselves saying, "I don't want to lose my sales job right now." Do some research and talk to trusted friends and colleagues to begin mapping out your options and getting more clear about what you DO want from your sales career.

- *Get your team together.* Whose support do you need to get your sales career back on track? Even having people around you to brainstorm ideas and get feedback on your options can be valuable. Start rekindling those relationships before you need them by reconnecting with old mentors, compatriots, and clients.

- *Know the lay of the land.* Good sales visionaries know what their customers want. They've figured out whether most sales are won on creativity or in the details, sales experience, computer or interpersonal skills. Then they work on the skills needed to give customers what they want.

- *Become an expert in a specific field.* As the old saying goes, you can learn a lot by watching. True enough. Watch and listen long enough, and you could soon become an expert in your field. Rather than sitting and waiting for someone to come along and proclaim them an expert, as too many sales professionals do, sales visionaries go out and become such experts. Whether it's going back to school to learn Excel, offering to write about it for an industry trade magazine, or even offering to talk about it in front of a Chamber of Commerce group, sales visionaries won't hesitate—and more importantly, aren't afraid—to become an industry expert. Imagine giving a speech on manufacturing-line innovations and impressing a potential customer in the audience—or maybe even better, impressing your future boss at a newer, better-paying, and more rewarding sales position.

- *Treat your career as a small business.* Sales visionaries take control of their own careers. They don't like leaving things to chance and possibly seeing someone else take control of their turf or their clients. Like the neighborhood grocer or that software startup out by the interstate, sales visionaries take their reputations and responsibilities personally. If clients aren't happy, sales visionaries learn that old small-business trick of "killing them with kindness" and making them happy customers once again. Also remember, thinking like a small-business owner enables you to react fast to problems.

- *Know your industry cold.* Sales visionaries can just about cite chapter and verse what their industry is up to on a daily basis. This sounds tough, especially for ultra-busy salespeople like single parents or professionals who volunteer in their community. However, all that becoming savvy about your industry entails is reading the industry newsletter or good blogs and newsletters online, or checking out *The Wall Street Journal* or *Business Week* or the industry trade publications that are invariably lying about the workplace. Even better is developing your own contacts in the industry and chatting them up once a week or so. The web is a big help, too. Industry associations almost always have websites chock full of information and data on your business. Or subscribe to an online clipping service that will e-mail you news and information on your business community. Lexus-Nexus (http://www.lexusnexus.com) and Northern Light (http://www.northernlight.com) are good places to start. So are Business Wire (http://www.businesswire.com) and PR Newswire (http://www.prnewswire.com).

- *Know the value of a mentor.* Sales visionaries align themselves with people who can champion their progress inside the executive boardroom. In a smaller business, this can be the chief executive officer (CEO) or the office administrator. In larger businesses, a mentor can be the director of one's own department—or another department—or simply a coworker who's got the ear of company decision makers or the ear of potential clients who might buy from you.

- *Develop a fat contact list.* Collecting business cards or e-mail addresses might seem like a waste of time to some people, but sales visionaries know that a phone number here or an e-mail address there can come in handy down the road. If you're attending a conference and don't have business cards to hand out or don't work hard to hand them out, you might be missing out on a bigger and better opportunity down the road. Contacts also come in handy when you are looking for good information on your industry. While nobody likes a pest, one thing I've learned in the sales business is that people love to talk if you give them a chance. Part of networking is also realizing what you can do for others. John F. Kennedy may have had patriotism on his mind when he famously spoke, "Ask not what your country can do for you, ask what you can do for your country." However, this is a line that translates well career-wise, too.

- *Tout your accomplishments—and the accomplishments of others.* It may seem ham-handed, even arrogant, but informing your boss and others of your successes and milestones is an important step toward meeting your sales destiny—and visibility does count. It's equally important to toot other people's horns occasionally. There is great power in a sincere compliment, and the favor invariably will be returned.

- *Stay ahead of the education curve.* Let's face it: we're in a global economy now where information is as much a commodity as compact disks or convertibles. Since technology changes seemingly on a daily basis, it is the savvy sales visionary who keeps up. This could mean taking that class in Web design if you're going to start your own business, or simply chatting up your coworkers for the latest trends in commerce and technology to help you better reach out to potential clients. Think of this as business insurance.

- *Know how to process feedback.* Listening is a lost art form and one that sales professionals who are serious about their careers should practice diligently. Therefore, make a vow to listen to what people at work or what clients are saying to you. You'll be surprised at how much you can learn about how people perceive you. Then work to make changes or—if the feedback is very positive—keep doing what you are doing. Also try to learn how to take feedback. If the feedback is positive, accept it by replying with a simple "Thank you." If the feedback is negative, don't fly off the handle or take it personally. Instead, hear the person out. If you believe the feedback is not accurate, ask for examples. If you see it as legitimate, respond with appreciation for having this pointed out to you. If you disagree with it, calmly and confidently state your position. Don't argue or become upset.

- *Recognize what you're worth.* Sales visionaries always know their value to their company, to their industry, and to potential employers in myriad industries. There is no shortage of surveys and annual reports on salaries in the workplace. Check them out to see where someone of your experience and position stands. Another good idea is to scout out the help-wanted ads (many include salary ranges these days) or contact an employment recruiter who's been around the block. Such a person can tell you what you're worth on the open market.

Not everything will work out exactly as you envision and you can't plan for every contingency, so be prepared to adapt as you go. Push forward with your sales career "destiny," but keep an eye on oncoming traffic and potential bumps in the road. Luckily, all the work you've done up to that point will ensure you're better able to handle any upcoming twists and turns on the way to your destination.

Q-Tip: *Feel Burnt Out? Try the "Memory" Tip*
The American Psychological Association defines burnout as "a depletion of an individual's energetic resources at work." Psychologists have linked burnout to increased risk for a range of health problems, including cardiovascular disease.

So how do you know if you're experiencing burnout? The Mayo Clinic, which is devoted to the diagnosis and treatment of virtually all complex illnesses, says these are some of the key signs:

- You find yourself being more cynical and sarcastic at work.
- You lack the energy to be consistently productive.
- You've become more irritable or less patient with coworkers and clients.
- You drag yourself into work and have trouble getting started once you arrive.
- You feel disillusioned about your job.
- You have a hard time laughing at yourself.

The key to recapturing that old enthusiasm for sales is to jog your memory bank and remember those passions. That will trigger a change in perspective. No doubt there are myriad challenges in the sales game.

So get those memories back by taking an afternoon and rereading those great letters your clients have written to you. Remember, those testimonials aren't just good marketing copy—they're a testament to your skills. This simple exercise can reignite your passion and get you excited about sales again.

Q-Tip: *Taking T-A-R-G-E-T Practice*

Setting targets is great, but it won't add up to much if you don't take action to meet those targets.

In my line of work, I hear lots of people talking the talk, but walking the walk? Not so much.

Actually, I'm a good example of that. I've been talking about writing a book for years—but I'm only now doing it.

On that note, use these tips as a roadmap—OK, GPS—to find career satisfaction.

T: Take stock of where you want to be—and how to get there.

A: Aim high—what have you got to lose? Take dead aim at the career you want; the career that awakens the passion inside of you.

R: Reinvent yourself as an in-demand commodity.

G: Grin and bear it. Stay positive; be an optimist. People love working with people who have a great outlook on life.

E: Excel at what you love to do. Identify your passion and then embrace it professionally. Life is short; why not live it making a living doing what you love to do?

T: Take time out to enjoy your family and friends—the ones that count appreciate you no matter what your career status.

Did you know that ten years after graduation, more than 80 percent of all college graduates are earning their living in fields completely unrelated to what they majored in at college?

In my mind, that fact underscores more than anything else I've ever heard the importance of setting long-term sales career goals.

I've applied the following broad guidelines to setting effective goals for the companies I've run. They apply equally well for sales professionals looking to jump-start their careers.

Do This	Not That
Do express your goals positively. "Execute this technique well" is a much better goal than "don't make this stupid mistake."	Don't take a negative tone. If you reinforce negative behavior, that's what you'll get.
Do Be Precise. If you set a precise goal, putting in dates, times, and amounts so that achievement can be measured, then you know the exact goal to be achieved, and can take complete satisfaction from having completely achieved it.	Don't make loose guesses. If your goals are loose, wide-ranging, and wobbly, your execution will be loose, wide-ranging, and wobbly.
Do set priorities. Where you have several goals, give each a priority. This helps you to avoid feeling overwhelmed by too many goals, and helps to direct your attention to the most important ones.	Don't wander from task to task. A disorganized sales professional is a failing sales professional. If you take a scattershot approach to your sales planning, you'll miss a lot more targets than you'll hit.
Do write goals down to avoid confusion and to give them more force.	Don't leave your best ideas in your head. You're busy and chances are you'll forget some of your pitch-perfect strategies.
Do keep operational goals small. Keep the goals you are working toward immediately (i.e., in this session) small and achievable. If a goal is too large, then it can seem that you are not making progress toward it. Keeping goals small and incremental gives more opportunities for reward. Today's goals should be derived from larger goals.	Don't overreach. The most ambitious plans can be overwhelming (and unappetizing) if you take too big a bite out of your sales career plan. Like your mother said, "everything in moderation."

Do This	Not That
Do . . . take pride in yourself and in your profession. Clients can smell uncertainty a mile away. If you're projecting an unconfident, less-than-professional image, you'll remain stuck in neutral.	*Don't . . . forget to listen. In my mind, the number one obstacle to sales success is not listening to what customers want. If you talk more than you listen, clients will walk more than they'll buy from you.*
Do . . . ask questions. Maybe you've forgotten the importance of asking customers what they want—but your customer hasn't. Make sure to prep some good questions in advance before you go see a client. By questioning, you separate suspects from prospects, find out customer needs and find out which of your products or services are suitable for them.	*Don't forget to show gratitude to your customer for spending time with you. Anytime you are with a customer you are in the right place.*

Above All, Do . . . visualize your sales success. Good visualization skills can help you recapture your sales magic. Try this exercise. Each morning, see yourself going out to see the customers and closing graciously. See your customers excitedly sign his purchase and looking forward to receiving the products. See the extra zeros on your paycheck. Above all, see yourself back in the driver's seat, closing sales and regaining your enthusiasm for the sales business.

Chapter Summary

How can you change your sales-career dynamic?

- **Take a personal inventory.** You can't get where you want to go unless you know where you are right now.

- **See yourself succeeding.** To get your sales mojo back, envision scenarios where you're connecting with clients and closing deals.

- **Know your destination.** See the path back to sales success as a journey, with your destination being a rejuvenated sales career.

- **Visualizing like a leader.** Big decision makers see the forest for the trees. Take some time, reflect, and visualize where you want to be in your sales career.

- **Verticalize your goals.** Take small, actionable steps to meet your goals. It can get discouraging to make big goals and then get over-whelmed and not reach them.

JUMP-START STEP #1:

Motivate Your Way To Sales Success

Let's have some fun and open the chapter with these quotes from one of my favorite films, *Glengarry Glen Ross*. The dialog points to a pair of key issues in sales—that it's time to wake up, and for in sales, failure is not an option.

Blake, played unforgettably by Alec Baldwin, is going *mano a mano* with Dave Moss, played by a superb Ed Harris. The subject? The art of the deal, and why Blake says he has it down but Dave Moss doesn't:

Blake: What's the problem, pal?

Dave Moss: You—

[*correcting him*]

Dave Moss: Moss. You're such a hero, you're so rich, how come you're coming down here wasting your time with such a bunch of bums?

Blake: You see this watch? You see this watch?

Dave Moss: Yeah.

Blake: That watch costs more than your car. I made $970,000 last year. How much did you make? You see, pal, that's who I am, and you're nothing. Nice guy? I don't give a [bleep]. Good father? [Bleep] you! Go home and play with your kids. You wanna work here—close! You think this is abuse? You think this is abuse, you [bleep]? You can't take this, how can you take the abuse you get on a sit? You don't like it, leave.

Blake [continuing]: You got leads. Mitch and Murray paid good money to get these names for you to sell them. You can't close the leads you're given, you can't close [bleep], *you are* [bleep)]. Hit the bricks pal, and beat it, 'cause you are going *out*.

Shelley Levene: The leads are weak.

Blake: "The leads are weak." The [bleeping] leads are weak? You're weak. I've been in this business fifteen years…

Dave Moss: What's your name?

Blake: [Bleep] you. That's my name.

[*Moss laughs*]

Blake: You know why, mister? 'Cause you drove a Hyundai to get here tonight, I drove an eighty-thousand-dollar BMW. [*Bleep*] you. That's my name.

The point that Baldwin's character indelicately makes is this: you need to motivate yourself to succeed. That's why I came up with the tagline "awakening the sales monster inside of you."

We all have that passion for sales, but in some of us, it burns out more quickly than it does in other people. The good news is this malady is pretty easily fixed—and we will tackle this in detail coming up in the Chapter.

Let's attack the root causes of lack of motivation by creating a composite character that can help us personalize the issue. I bet our sales avatar will remind you of someone you know in sales, if not yourself.

Let's call him "Bob."

A successful medical-supply sales representative whose nickname in his salad days was "Bonus Check Bob," he had hit hard times, laid low by a tough economy and a gradual disinterest in the profession he had embraced since starting out as a sales rep right out of college. The once hungry and hardscrabble top producer had seemingly lost his touch and had grown indifferent to a sales culture that seemed to value faxes, e-mails, and cell-phone chats instead of the face-to-face relationship building he'd excelled at. Worse, he'd lost his passion for the sales business and forgot the reasons he got into the business in the first place: the face-to-face interaction, the thrill of closing a deal, the satisfaction of building long-term relationships.

It was a strange feeling for someone who had always felt easily at home in the sales world.

After all, Bob had the classic sales background, didn't he? Bob had started in grade school, selling candy door-to-door, buying them for a quarter and selling them for fifty cents to hungry moms and dads and to kids who had allowance money that was burning holes in their pockets. He grew more involved in sales in high school, where he took a part-time job after school selling baby pictures to proud parents—especially mothers—in his town. Bob learned, through trial and error, that he could package the pictures in such a way that people usually purchased the set he wanted them to buy. By asking a proud mom whether she wanted the bargain package or the value package, Bob found that most of his customers would opt for the more expensive value package. Nobody wanted to skimp on their baby pictures, and he learned that people buy on emotions.

Bob dabbled in sales all through college, selling tie-dyed shirts and ties to fellow students on the campus concourse at Penn State University and later marketing "Florida Break" spring vacations for a local travel agent, who gave Bob 50 percent of the cut for bringing her the business.

After college he went right to work selling ad time for a big-city radio station and later switched to medical-supply sales after a company Bob touted to his investor clients made her an offer he couldn't refuse. There, he learned the art of sales—the importance of developing a network of contacts that could, like his travel-agent boss, bring him business. Bob learned about how to keep himself sharp with cold calls, but cold calls proved inefficient compared with building a network of trusted customers over time. He trained himself to focus on developing healthy client relationships that lasted for the long term. After all, those accounts comprised 85 percent of his sales. Bob found that, even in tough times when customers were buying less, it was the sales representative with the best contacts and the best relationships—and not the "quick hit" artist—who survived and thrived.

Before long, Bob had forged for himself a six-figure annual income and plenty of trips to exotic ports of call for exceeding his quotas, and he even found time to have a reasonable home and social life. For the next several years, he was on Cloud Nine.

But that was then and this was now. Fatigue, restlessness, and a vague sense of unhappiness had slowly enveloped him in recent months. He'd tried to talk to his wife about his fatigue and then his boss. Bob told both that he was burnt out; that he dreaded coming to work in the morning and how making his calls and traveling through his territory—a weekly practice he'd always found enjoyable—now felt like drudgery. Bob even began feeling cynical about his boss and his company—something he dared not bring up to anybody.

Boxed in, Bob started to feel like there was no hope—that he was in it for the money and couldn't recapture that "lightning in a bottle" magic he'd had for sales when he'd started out in sales.

But what if Bob had a foolproof system to turn his situation—better yet, his life—around? What if he had a formula for regaining his enthusiasm for sales that he could turn to again and again, and use to awaken the sales monster inside of him?

What Bob needed was a "jump start" to get moving—and you can use the tips in this book too.

Getting Fired Every Day? It's a Good Thing

Somebody asked me how I got to be such a good salesman. I felt humbled, but I had an answer. I tell myself every night that I've lost my job and tomorrow I have to start from scratch. With that thought in mind, I always treated every day like my first day at work—I was out to show people what I could do.

Tapping into "Hidden" Energy

What can we do to get Bob back on track—and the rest of us in the process?

With a fresh start—a "reawakening" if you will, that's how.

I believe that there is more than one way to look at the challenge of getting the most out of your sales career. In Bob's case, it was a new way to look at sales that he—and you—had likely never seen before.

That what I hope makes this book both informative and, I believe, fun to read. That's important me, as a guy who's had the privilege of building businesses and a sales career—a sales career that I assure you has been fun and profitable. I've also enjoyed working with many successful salespeople in all different stages of their careers—and I've learned a lot from all of them in the process. Two themes I've taken away in particular from the great sales pros I've met are the stages of career satisfaction (or "happiness") with what they have accomplished, and their level of optimism about their futures.

I have specifically noticed clear plateaus in the "energy" of these salespeople that I've have worked with. Although all career choices present challenges for sustaining success, it seems to me that sales professionals in particular are constantly measured against very rigid, economically driven barometers and exposed to constant internal and external competition.

Consequently, like our friend Bob found out, our feelings of frustration and harmful stress run very high in the sales industry. The cost to sales organizations in lost talent, rehiring, and retraining negatively impacts the corporate bottom line. Unfortunately, but unmistakably, the emotional toll of high stress can be devastating to any sales professional's career.

In my experience, sales professionals don't always acknowledge that pressure. Or, if they do, they internalize it and cover it up. That's a big mistake. While most salespeople are well schooled in the nuts and bolts of the selling process, there seems to be something missing for them that can cause a loss of optimism and premature burnout.

The key is to hit that "reset" button and take fresh stock of your career, i.e. where it's been, where it is now, and where it's headed into the future.

By "hitting the reset button," I simply mean looking at sales opportunities in new ways.

For example, while working on a project that focused on sales-force effectiveness, I began the warm-up by telling the salespeople about when I worked for a big company in the 1980s. One day we were visited by the new sales manager, who gathered us around the twelfth-floor window looking out across the Philadelphia skyline. He pointed at buildings and asked, "Who is in that building?" None of us knew. The sales manager then tapped one of us on the shoulder and instructed that person to find out. He did this several times. This was a memorable lesson in "cold-calling." You need to look right in front of you and create opportunities.

That's what I mean about awakening the sales monster inside of you—to trigger new ways to look at old challenges. That's the heart and soul of my "Awaken the Monster" sales success system—and I want you to learn it, too.

To Blake, sales are all about awakening the sales monster that all of us have inside, and then identifying opportunities and wasting no time in going after them.

Lay the Groundwork for Success

A great writer once confessed that the most self-motivating tool for him was a blank piece of paper in his typewriter. So he developed a plan to tackle the potential problem. Each day, when he was ready to quit writing, he would leave a piece of paper in the typewriter with a sentence half-finished on it. The next morning, the first thing he would do was finish that sentence. Soon he would be thoroughly engrossed in his writing—and off to a productive day.

Seven Traits You'll Need to Come Back from the Brink—and Cash in on Your Passion for Sales

The people who best survive sales career setbacks are the ones with fires in their bellies—the ones who, deep down inside, believe that the future is now and that the next sale is right around the corner.

Usually, they possess most or all of the following character traits:

1. **Believe in Yourself.** If you want to be a successful sales monster, you must learn to trust your instincts and ideas. You must be willing to be persistent, determined, self-confident, and disciplined, from start to finish. As you become wiser and more confident, you'll find that your belief in yourself grows stronger as well. You need desire and passion to start the journey toward your meeting your sales goals. Think of believing in yourself and your ideas as the vehicle for getting to your destination.

2. **Think Creatively.** Don't be afraid to think creatively. Many people get frustrated because their thinking involves sales-improvement ideas that already exist. That shouldn't stop you. Instead, you should think of ways to improve, expand, and enhance existing ideas. "Thinking outside the box" is a well-worn cliché, but entrepreneurs and upper-level managers know it's true and adopt it as a motto. They put their imagination to work to try new things and work toward a vision. To be a successful creative thinker, pay close attention to how well your sales strategies are working, and be willing to change your approach if you find something isn't working well.

3. **Explore and Use Your Skills.** Successful salespeople know they aren't good at everything; instead, they focus on the things they can do exceptionally well. By evaluating your own skills, you can determine those that will help you work toward your goals. Creative thinkers are also willing to let other experts in to help with things they aren't as good at. Staying open to change is important so that an entrepreneur can move forward and continue to be successful.

4. Create and Follow A Plan. To achieve success, you must follow a plan. You wouldn't take a road trip without a map, and you shouldn't expect to reach your professional sales destinations without a guide to follow. Along the way, you might find that another road seems more appealing and effective, but you wouldn't have reached that point without an initial plan. By all means, take detours if you must—but always make sure you have a plan for reaching your goal. Start out by writing a basic business plan that will guide you and your accomplishments. Don't worry about making it elaborate or long, but make sure you include goals, ideas, ways you'll be better than the competition, and ideas for marketing. You should make sure to update your plan according to your new ideas.

5. Envision Your Success. Remember how they told you not to daydream in school? Ignore that advice. Take time to envision your final sales goals. You'll find that the visualization is a powerful motivator. Athletes routinely envision how they want each performance to play out, and it helps them achieve their sporting goals. Imagine how you want things to turn out and how good you'll feel as a successful entrepreneur; it will help make your dreams seem like a more tangible reality.

6. Respect Your Peers. The old saying "To have a friend, be a friend" rings true in the business world too. Recognize everyone you meet as a peer deserving your respect, and you'll find that these people return the favor. You'll never know if someone you meet could become part of your rejuvenated sales career. Smart sales types let others work with them to the best of their abilities, giving everyone the chance to reach personal goals. The success of your team relies on each person's contributions. By putting others on an equal level, you'll find that they respect you back and give you their best performance.

7. Don't Give Up. To cash in on sales success, don't give up on your dreams. This doesn't mean successful individuals don't have discouraging moments, bad days, and disappointments, but they see these as part of the journey, not as the end. Successful sales types must have the determination to overcome these difficulties, and this determination is the result of self-trust and self-confidence. Smart "sales survivors" know that when the chips are down, they should turn to people who know them and their ability to succeed, for these people will offer encouragement and put them enthusiastically back on track. In order to be successful, you must accept the ebb and flow of good and bad periods. This will keep you going long after others have given up in frustration.

Q-Tip: *Another Anecdote on Looking at Problems in New Ways*

Where some salespeople see disaster, others see opportunity.

There were three stores in a row. One day the owner of the right-hand store put up a sign: "FIRE SALE."

The man on the left end, not to be outdone, put up a sign: "BANKRUPTCY SALE."

The man in the middle was stymied for a while. Then he came out with a sign: "MAIN ENTRANCE."

Motivating Yourself

I'm all about motivating one's self—especially the part about leveraging that "monster" inside of you and using it as a motivator to capitalize on sales opportunities.

I know, I've experienced it myself.

A few years ago, I was on a sales call. It was a big client with great name recognition and I really wanted the sale. After about an hour and a half of rapport building, presenting, questioning, and empathizing, I left the client's office with a lukewarm response to my closing questions. I felt discouraged and frustrated. Another wasted call—and half a day to boot. But what I had come to realize and what has saved me from dejection after such sales calls was the new mindset I had adapted: that I had just planted a seed—that I was not after a sale as much as I was after another opportunity to plant a seed. I really did not have to brace myself any longer—I knew that if I followed up on that call—really took care of the freshly planted seed—that the business would turn my way. Sure enough, I lost the original sale—but two years later, this account became one of my biggest revenue generators.

The experience really motivated me. I started focusing on "seeding" those opportunities. The more seeds I planted, the happier I felt. I was spreading the word about my cleaning business, getting deeper into my customers' business. I wasn't after a sale as much as a new opportunity and chance to plant a seed. It really took the stress off my shoulders and I came across to my customers in a more relaxed, natural way. I think they enjoyed talking with me more, and that's what it's about for me, enjoying the process.

From there, my mission to attack new opportunities grew easier. I really started targeting my best opportunities; taking time to assess their needs carefully, planning two or three calls per day instead of six so I could really get in-depth on customer needs. These activities surely beat my old routine, which had digressed to daily keeping track of where I stood on the last sales contest, or calculating my commissions over and over based on different product combinations.

Before I knew it, I was doing it on a regular basis and my customers were responding to it. I felt like I had really found something different, and I began getting the old Mojo back.

Awakening yourself means knowing WHAT makes you passionate about selling, and WHO you really want to spend your time with as a customer. That's it in a nutshell...and without that opportunistic mindset, you're just selling anything you can to anybody that will buy...and that's a recipe for eventual burnout.

My takeaway? I really do believe motivation is the driving force in sales—it always conjures up all kinds of opportunities when you see a highly motivated sales professional in action.

Back in the day, there was a highly successful company called Quill Corporation, based out of Chicago. They sold a lot of office supplies and had a real maverick of a founder and chief executive officer named Jack Miller. He was one of the first salesmen to hook up all of his 650,000 customers to an online ordering system (and this was way back in the 1980s). Here's the beauty part: Miller even charged $14.95 just to place an order. But clients were so happy to order office supplies in thirty seconds or less—they barely noticed.

That's what I mean when I say you have to be creative and alert about identifying opportunities—often they're right there in front of you. All you have to do is grab them.

The "Birdseye" View: Always Be Looking for Opportunity

If you are fishing at twenty degrees below zero and you pull a big fish up through the ice, an obvious thing happens. The fish freezes, fast and hard. But Clarence Birdseye, grinding out a living as a fur trader in Labrador in the years leading up to World War I, noted something not-so-obvious about these quickly frozen fish.

When thawed, the fish were actually tender and flaky—and very tasty. It was almost as good as eating fresh fish, he thought. The same was true for other frozen game, like caribou, elk, and geese. Even heads of cabbage tasted great after storing them outside is cabin during a long Canadian winter.

That observation made Clarence Birdseye a wealthy man. The quick-freezing process engineered by Birdseye produced frozen foods that busy families loved to eat. It also gave farmers the incentive to grow crops for a year-round market.

Birdseye later said, "There was nothing remarkable in what I had done." And that's my point exactly—you don't have to create magic to succeed in sales— you just have to recognize opportunity when you see it.

How to Awaken That Sales Monster Inside of You: Some Tips

Now I want you to learn how to motivate yourself—or "awaken" like Bob did earlier in this chapter—and start capturing some of those great opportunities.

Let's start with some tips to awaken that sales monster I'm talking about. They've worked for me and they'll work for you.

- **Decide You're Going to Win in Sales**: Make a decision to go all the way to the top of your field. Make a decision today to join the top 10 percent. There is no one and nothing that can hold you back from being the best except yourself.

- **Work on Your Weakest Points**: Identify your weakest single skill and make a plan to become absolutely excellent in that area. Ask yourself, and your boss, *"What one skill, if I developed and did it consistently in an excellent fashion, would have the greatest positive impact on my sales?"* Whatever your answer to this question, write it down, set a deadline, make a plan, and then work on it every day.

- **Hang with Winners:** Get around positive, successful people. Associate with men and women who are going somewhere with their lives. And get away from negative, critical, complaining people. Remember, you cannot fly with the eagles if you continue to scratch with the turkeys.

- **Work on Your Physical Health:** Take excellent care of your physical health. You need high levels of energy to sell effectively and to bounce back from continual rejection and discouragement. Be sure to eat the right foods, get the right amount of exercise, and get plenty of rest and recreation.

- **Practice positive self-talk continually.** Control your inner dialogue. Talk to yourself the way you want to be rather than the way you might be today.

- **Take positive action toward your goals, every single day**. Be proactive rather than reactive. Grab the bull by the horns. If you are not happy with your income, get out there and get face-to-face with more customers.

I really want to drive this point home. To awaken the sales genius that's most definitely inside of you, you have to push your sales career into higher gear. That means motivating yourself, that means demanding more of yourself, and that means owning your future in sales.

Believe me, it's out there. And it's just waiting for you to grab it by the neck and own it for yourself.

Q-Tip: *Inspirational Quotes on Making the Most of Your Sales Opportunities*

When defeat comes, accept it as a signal that your plans are not sound, rebuild those plans, and set sail once more toward your coveted goal.

Napoleon Hill

You are never too old to set another goal or to dream a new dream.

C. S. Lewis

Leaders aren't born, they are made. And they are made just like anything else, through hard work. And that's the price we'll have to pay to achieve that goal, or any goal.

Vince Lombardi

All successful people men and women are big dreamers. They imagine what their future could be, ideal in every respect, and then they work every day toward their distant vision, that goal or purpose.

Brian Tracy

Never quit. It is the easiest cop-out in the world. Set a goal and don't quit until you attain it. When you do attain it, set another goal, and don't quit until you reach it. Never quit.

Bear Bryant

Desire is the key to motivation, but it's determination and commitment to an unrelenting pursuit of your goal—a commitment to excellence—that will enable you to attain the success you seek.

Mario Andretti

Q-Tip: *Sales Slump? Keep a Cool Head*

If you're in a sales slump, don't get mad—get motivated.

Frustration and anger can be misinterpreted by your clients, peers, and managers as being emotional or out of control. When you're in a slump more than at any other time, you need to be totally in control and assure others around you that you know exactly what to do. Whenever you find yourself becoming angry, try to be as honest as possible, and focus on solutions and options—not on laying blame.

Do This	Not That
Do . . . take a personal inventory of yourself, and use the information revealed to leverage a "reawakening" into a new, revitalized career path.	*Don't . . . assume that you can plod along without a plan to re-energize your sales career. What form that takes is up to you—a vacation, a job switch, or even a move to a new industry.*
Do . . . jack up your sales mojo by identifying new opportunities to make new sales—and more importantly, build new relationships.	*Don't . . . try to transform your career on your own. Like you can highly benefit from a trusted friend or professional to bounce ideas off of, and to guide you down a path where you're re-engaged in your own sales career.*

Above All, Do . . . watch your top clients and apply what works for them to the rest of your client base. Not every client is perfect, but the few who are can help you understand how to "reawaken" a winning formula—and identify future winning opportunities down the road.

Chapter Summary

How can you awaken that sales monster inside of you—and use that motivation to create and identify new sales opportunities?

- You can't get where you want to go unless you know where you are right now.

- To get your sales mojo back, envision scenarios where you're connecting with clients and closing deals.

- See the path back to sales success as a journey, with your destination being a rejuvenated sales career.

JUMP-START STEP #2:

Find—and Master - Opportunity

Opportunities come and go—the trick is to recognize them when they are in front of you and make the most of them.

Back in the late 1930s, an Eastern Airlines crew member entered the Marriott Hotel coffee shop down the road from the airport in Washington, DC. He asked for a quart of hot coffee to go.

The waitress asked, "Are you driving to New York?"

The young airline employee said, "No, we're flying there. We'll drink the coffee on the way."

The waitress cheerfully filled his thermos with coffee. "Come back any time—we'll make sure you're stocked up—and don't forget to tell your friends," she said.

The airline worker did—and soon more airline employees were stopping by the coffee shop before flying—picking up coffee, sandwiches, and candy bars for their flights. The manager of the coffee shop couldn't help but notice, and told Bill Marriott, the head of the hotel chain. A savvy businessman, Marriott called the president of Eastern Airlines the next day and offered him a deal—and airlines have been serving in-flight meals from Marriott ever since.

Turns out, Bill Marriott knew what all great salespeople know; that to awaken the sales monster that all of us have inside, we have to identify opportunities and waste no time in going after them.

Opening the Door When Opportunity Knocks

A while back, one of my neighbors told me that after almost thirty years building a steady sales career with a major financial services firm, he had hit the wall and needed advice on how to beef up his prospecting program.

That really surprised me: this is a guy who, for three decades, enjoyed his job and made great money doing it. Now, late in his career, he finds himself looking to get his game face back, looking for an answer to how he could energize his prospecting.

Even with the stagnant economy, my friend knew that there were sales opportunities out there. He was in insurance sales and people still needed coverage—especially if they got sick or lost their jobs.

So what did I tell him? Try these tips, for starters:

- **Plan to Identify Opportunities**. Craft a written business plan on how you will identify sales opportunities. Be specific with details that include all the aspects of your prospecting activity and then review the business plan with someone who is qualified to determine that the objectives are both realistic and attainable.

- **Mentor up.** Whether you are new to the business or are an experienced veteran, try to partner—or at a minimum, create a strategic marketing alliance—with someone who is successful and experienced in the targeted market segment you are interested in. The successful person has already established the prospecting techniques that can serve as a model for you.

- **Watch Your Top Clients.** I know. It would be great if all our clients were happy and easy to please. Why are your best customers so great? And how can you mold your other clients in the same light? Start by evaluating what makes those good clients so great. What are the traits they have in common? Direct your marketing campaign to people who are just like them. Focus on their niche! You'll net new consumers and higher profits for your efforts.

- **Let Your Clients Know That Time Is a Commodity, Too.** Likely, sales clients these days are busy. They're in a hurry, and will strike a good deal if they think they can get a good product or service and save a buck or two in the process. How much do you think they would appreciate the ability to do both in your shop? Identify the opportunity and then capitalize on it by emphasizing the time they'll save and the money they'll keep in their pockets while enjoying all of the wonderful benefits your products have to offer. Kick in some discounts where they can save even more cash (with a deadline, of course). When people can save time and money on a deal, your sales numbers will rise in the process.

- **Easy Does It.** Convenience is the key to attracting buyers in today's rough-and-tumble economy. Finding out what customers want in the buying process is an opportunity just waiting to happen. Think about it—easy access is why convenience stores do so well.

- **Get the Good Word Out.** Let friends, colleagues, and family members know you are actively seeking new clients and offer incentives to them for recommending you. You can give them certificates to their favorite stores, tickets to a play, a trip to a spa, or a small percentage of the signing fee.

- **Track Your Progress.** Since your time is precious, you can't afford to waste it on ineffective marketing tactics. And you will only know which tactics are effective by tracking their results. Track exactly how many clients come in from each marketing tactic, and use only the ways that are most efficient.

- **Use Social Networking.** While it's still useful to create and distribute brochures and other materials that describe you and your firm, I'm a big believer in using well-traveled social networking sites like Facebook and Twitter to keep customers in the loop—and help identify new ones. They tell potential clients what you do, how you do it, why you're good at it, and the types of clients you work with. The best social networking "messages" come from the clients' points of view and always tell prospective customers what's in it for them.

- **Spread Your Wings.** Be a joiner and get involved with professional associations, giving speeches, or teaching a course. This will elevate your credibility and stature in the field and introduce you to people who may need your services. Speaking at seminars and workshops helps get you recognized as an expert in your field, enhances your reputation, and increases your visibility. All this adds up to a larger pool of potential customers.

- **Volunteer Yourself.** Getting involved with community groups, sitting on boards of directors for nonprofits, or performing volunteer work can help introduce you to influential people, both in and out of your line of work. If you make the right impression, these people could be potential clients or referral sources.

- **Follow Up.** No doubt about it, future opportunities lie in good sales follow-ups—even the sales you lose! I've found that following up can be the determining factor between a rejection and a satisfied, loyal customer. Simply contact them afterwards and let them know the product is still available or offer them further information that he or she may find valuable.

Q-Tip: *Seizing Opportunities the John Glenn Way*

Opportunity should be taken full advantage of.

Case in point. Astronaut John Glenn realized that the first astronaut would be the one the world would remember. He dreamed up a scheme to improve his chances of being the first selected.

While a major in the US Marines, Glenn decided to make a coast-to-coast flight at an average speed of Mach 1. Everyone who knew about air travel knew that it could be done. But nobody bothered to do it until Glenn—the first astronaut ever—bothered to do it.

Case Study: Enthusiasm Can Turn Losers into Winners

I've always been firm on the subject of passion and sales. My clients may not have always known that, but my co-workers did. I'm a big believer in passion. In fact, I believe passion can turn losers into winners.

When Vince Lombardi took over the Green Bay Packers, they were at the bottom of the league. In 1958 they lost just about all of their games. When they returned to training camp in summer, 1959, the Packers were greeted by their new coach.

Lombardi told him players the following: "Gentlemen, we are going to have a football team. We are going to win games. Get that?"

"How are we going to do that? We are going to learn how to block, run, and tackle. You are going to outplay all of the teams that come up against you."

Lombardi then closed the sale. "You are going to have confidence in me and enthusiasm for my system—and for each other. I want you to think of three things: your home, your family, and the Green Bay Packers.

In the next ten years, the Packers would use that passion to win six championships, including the first two Super Bowls.

I loved that story; how Lombardi understood the power of passion. It's what enabled Noah Webster to spend thirty-six years on his dictionary, what kept George Stephenson working for fifteen years on his locomotive, what saw Thomas Edison endure ten thousand defeats before perfecting the incandescent lamp, and what drove Cyrus W. Field to endure nearly thirteen years of ceaseless toil before he finally laid the Atlantic ocean cable. These guys never quit and I won't either, and neither should you.

Now let that enthusiasm take hold of you, because that's where it all starts!

Three Keys To "Awakening" Your Sales Career

1. Craft a formula for success. In other words, have an action plan.

2. Execute the plan clearly and compellingly.

3. Crave information—knowledge feeds the sales beast.

Identifying Why Customers Say "No" to You

Sure, we'd all like to live in a sun-drenched world where everyone bought from us—no question asked.

Sorry, but that's not happening. People tend to say "no" a lot. What we do when people say no—what we learn from the experience—is an opportunity all its own.

I call it the "power of no." When customers reject us, we need to know why. Whether it's an excuse, a justification, or an obstacle that leads a potential client away from you, identifying and overcoming these objections is crucial to growing your business.

So how do you identify the reasons behind an objection? Mainly by listening. If you really hear what your customer is saying—and equally important—what he's not saying.

There are a few specific areas where you should focus, and where you should identify why your client is in rejection mode—and what you can to reverse the situation, thus creating a new opportunity to close the deal.

Use these questions if you can't get past the dreaded word "no"

- What is your biggest concern?

- Can you explain why this worries you?

- What would be the ideal outcome?

- What is your priority with this project?

- What are the primary factors in your decision?

Be patient when you ask these questions, and don't be shy about taking notes—it shows you care about what the client is saying. Above all else, stay positive. As the old saying goes, when one door closes, another one opens.

Q-Tip: *What are some typical reasons why clients say "no" to us? Here's a list of some of the most common ones:*

- **Price**: "Your services cost too much. I can get the 'same' service from someone cheaper."

- **Fear of Change:** "I don't want to change the way we've been doing things for fifteen years. Too much can go wrong."

- **Trust:** "It seems like you know what you're doing, but how do I know you really have the necessary experience to do this?"

- **Personal Politics:** "I told my friend's brother's son's wife I'd use her company for my next project."

- **External Input:** "I need to run this by my wife/business partner/ friend before I do anything else."

- **Timing:** "It's too much for me to take on right now; I don't have time to fulfill my responsibilities in this arrangement."

> You'll need a good answer for each of these concerns, if and when your client brings them up. Don't assume these issues won't come up—they will. It's up to you to be ready when they do.

Taking Action Reaps Big Rewards

Opportunity is waiting for you, but you have to make it happen.

Alexander Graham Bell, inventor of the telephone, is said to have beat another to the patent office by ten minutes.

Case Study: Overcoming Negativity: The Hot Dog Man Story

While a positive attitude added is the foundation on which a sales career rejuvenation can take flight, a negative one will just as surely reduce one's chances of sustaining that success.

There's a great story about how a negative attitude can derail the greatest sales career prospects, called "The Man Who Sold Hot Dogs." In it, a 1930s-era man lived by the side of the road and sold hot dogs. He was hard of hearing so he had no radio. He had no formal education so he couldn't read. But he sold great hot dogs.

He spent his days standing at the side of the road hollering, "Buy a hot dog, mister?" And people did. So many did, in fact, that he doubled and then tripled his bun and hot dog orders. He built a nice roof for his stand so people could eat his hot dogs in the rain or snow. He grew so busy that he called on his son, recently home from college, to help out.

But his son didn't want any part of selling hot dogs. He told his father, "Dad, don't you read the papers or listen to the radio? There's a war brewing in Europe and we're in a recession at home. Things are terrible all over." Thinking the son, being a college graduate, must know what he was talking about, the man reduced his hot dog orders and pulled back on his bun deliveries. He took down his roof and sold the spare parts. Soon he stopped selling hot dogs by the side of the road altogether. Naturally his bank account dwindled and debts piled up in his mailbox.

The father said to his son, "You know, son, you were right. We are in the middle of a great depression."

So don't let other people's negative attitudes poison your own. Keep your own course and stay positive. Believe me, it will get you noticed.

Q-Tip: *Keep an Open Mind*

Opportunity is everywhere—if you have an open mind.

A bright young man entered the employment office of a large company and asked for a job he'd seen advertised.

The manager said, "But young man, you're much too late. We've already received one thousand applications.

The young man answered, "Well, how about hiring me to screen the applications?"

Chapter Summary

How can you awaken that sales monster inside of you—and use that motivation to create and identify new sales opportunities?

- Seize any opportunity you can. Every day.

- To get your sales mojo back, envision scenarios where you're connecting with clients and closing deals.

- See the path back to sales success as a journey, with your destination being a rejuvenated sales career.

JUMP-START STEP 3

Knowledge is Power: The Sage of the "Five Monkeys"

Did you ever hear the story about the "Five Monkeys"?

It centers on an experiment that started with five monkeys in a cage. A banana was hung inside the cage with a set of steps placed underneath it. After a while, a monkey went to the steps and started to climb toward the banana, but when he touched the steps, he set off a spray that soaked all the other monkeys with cold water. Another monkey tried to reach the banana with the same result. It didn't take long for the monkeys to learn that the best way to stay dry was to prevent any monkey from attempting to reach the banana.

The next stage of the experiment was to remove the spray from the cage and to replace one of the monkeys with a new one. Of course, the new monkey saw the banana and went over to climb the steps. To his horror, the other monkeys attacked him. After another attempt, he learned that if he touched the steps, he would be assaulted.

Next, another of the original five was replaced with a new monkey. The newcomer went to the steps and was attacked. The previous newcomer joined in the attack with enthusiasm.

Then, a third monkey was replaced with a new one and then a fourth. Every time a newcomer approached the steps, he was attacked. Most of the monkeys beating him had no idea why they were not allowed to climb the steps or why they were joining in the beating of the newest monkey.

After the fifth monkey was replaced, none of the monkeys had ever been sprayed with water. Still, no monkey ever approached the steps.

Why not? Because as far as they knew, it was the way it had always been done around here…and that is how most corporate sales programs begin.

Q-Tip: *Custer's Last Stand*

General Custer lost the battle at Little Big Horn, but did he do so because of poor information and his own assumptions?

From June 25th to June 26th in 1876, Custer and his Seventh Cavalry attacked and battled with the Cheyenne Indians in Montana with poor information. First, Custer was given false information on how many Indians were actually at Little Big Horn. The Indian agents who provided Custer with the information based their numbers on nothing more than a guess. Indian agents came up with numbers by using the estimated number of Indians who were forced off their reservations and who was left; they didn't even account for those who were kicked off reservations and didn't leave.

Like most people in sales, Custer actually did have a goal. According to Custer historians, the general's goal was to contain the Indian population at Little Big Horn, not fight with them.

But what he lacked was some good risk analysis. If General Custer and his cavalry had worked more closely with Indian agents and asked some prudent questions to evaluate any threats in their goal to contain the Indians at Little Big Horn, Custer and many of his soldiers might have not lost their lives.

It's All About Learning

I've been in sales situations where the sales professional reminded me of one of those monkeys—making ill-informed decisions and growing more and more comfortable with the status quo—just like those lab monkeys did.

In my mind it's all about one of the most overlooked areas of sales—the learning aspect.

As both a veteran of the sales wars and the head of my own company, I place a very high premium on learning. In my book, if you're not curious and if you have no interest in learning something new, then you're not really trying.

You're also probably not cut out for a career in sales.

But if you do have the unquenchable thirst for knowledge, then learning about sales and selling can not only be a career saver, it can be a lot of fun, too.

Myself, I like to read a lot. While there's no substitute for meeting someone in person and sizing them up for a potential sale, you then get the bigger picture about effective sales strategies by reading—by learning—and then acting on the information you've absorbed.

For example, I am currently reading an e-book that is teaching me some very useful information on applying the proper techniques to make sales. It's all about learning to "prepare" to sell. From time to time, I've said in this book that preparing is a key element to a successful sale, specifically preparing by learning all you can about your customer. Sure, you can pound away at a new set of hinges all you want, but people likely won't respond to the actual product (the hinges). Instead, they want to learn about you—to read into the way you are presenting the product or service by your personal tics, traits, and tendencies.

Makes sense to me. So why wouldn't we take the time to learn about our customers, to learn about the best ways to reach out and connect to them?

That's why my personal mantra on selling is this: do your homework, learn all you can about the product or service you are going to sell. The more informed you are, the better prepared you are to answer your customers questions and concerns. Remember, pre-selling is the key to your success. That bond you create will pay off in customer satisfaction and repeat sales. Repeat sales equals the steady income stream I have talked about throughout this book.

Look, it's not rocket science. After all, any effective closer knows that he or she should pay close attention to the approaches, personalities, and tactics of anyone else sharing in his or her craft. Whether it is the small business owner who prints t-shirts on the Jersey Shore boardwalk or the painter looking to paint your house, we can learn something from everyone we meet.

Information is the seed for an idea, and it grows whenever it's watered.

—*HEINZ V. BERGEN*

Who Can You Learn From?

You can't go wrong following the tenets of Albert Einstein.

But it's one line from Einstein that I particularly like—"information is power."

Consequently, the message for this chapter is a single one: NEVER stop acquiring information. After all, information can only be empowering if you keep acquiring it (or keep "feeding the sales monster inside of you," as it were).

Job one to get your information-gathering campaign rolling is to figure out the best people you can learn from.

For a sales professional, that list is short, but ever-so-vital.

Here's a quick list:

Who Can You Learn From in Sales?

Customers: There may be no better source of instruction (and inspiration) than learning from your own customers. Who better? Your customer is a fountain of knowledge for closing sales—a direct path to more sales. In particular, watch out for signals from your customer on what he or she needs to grow their business. It might even be something beyond your product line, like a referral for a good tax advisor or just a broad conversation on how to grow their business. As always, listening and asking the right questions are the best ingredients for an information-gathering campaign from your customer.

Lost Customers: "How did I lose that piece of business?" It's an age-old question in the sales game. But learning how you lost business is a huge factor in winning more business. So go ahead and call your old customers and ask them what it was that caused them to go in another direction. The answer to that question is likely the same answer to what you need to do to grab new customers—only in reverse.

Competitors: Chances are, there is someone in your industry who, year-after-year, possesses a track record of success, and who has a sales model you can learn from. You might see this sales monster at industry events, at social gatherings, or even on sales calls as you're coming and he or she is going. Don't be afraid to stop that person and set a date on your calendars to meet and discuss the sales industry and what each of you are doing to gain maximum leverage. You may not get all of their secrets, but meeting over drinks or coffee may open up another invaluable source of information that can help you kick your sales engine into overdrive.

Industry Associations: When it comes to information, there is strength in numbers. That's why you should widen your potential pool of learning sources by joining as many industry associations as possible. Check their websites for articles and commentary, download their web casts, and avail yourself to as many conferences and seminars as possible. The more you know about your industry—and the more people you know in it—the better and stronger your knowledge base.

When you're working with any of the above learning resources, make sure to ask the right questions. Start with these questions first:

➢ Who are you doing business with right now—and why?

➢ If it's your customers, ask what you're doing right—and wrong.

➢ Also, ask how you can improve.

➢ How does your knowledge source prefer to be sold to?

➢ What's the most effective mode of communication for your knowledge source?

Whenever you engage a potential knowledge source, always try to learn something new and different every time out. That will set the stage for a fresh and revitalized view of your sales process—from the perspective of people who can really help you out.

One other key point - when you do lose a sale, and we all do, strive to figure out why you didn't get the piece of business, don't make the mistake of assuming it's price that was the reason why in the end.

It's not price. More likely, it's YOU—your message, your communications skills, the way you carry yourself. So when you do your due diligence after you lose a sale, make sure you follow up and ask that customer what YOU can do to next time to gain their trust—and their business.

....

Intelligence is the ability to adapt to change.

—*Stephen Hawking*

....

Learning something new can mean the difference between success and failure in sales.

Let me give you an example.

We're living in the information age, where knowledge is just as much a commodity as ball bearings or big-screen televisions. So as sales professionals, we want to learn how to transmit knowledge faster and more efficiently.

I have a business acquaintance in the computer software field. He recently told me something interesting—that his company increased sales by 20 percent in one month (one month!) simply by using Twitter.

I'll leave the name of the company blank to protect my friend's professional identity, but here's how they did it.

The sixty-person company headquartered in Los Angeles is an SEO (search engine optimization) marketing software firm that's been in business for fifteen years. They rely mostly on word-of-mouth advertising and have just two people who do marketing (one of whom is devoted to SEO); almost everyone else provides customer service.

But their sole marketing specialist had been on Twitter personally since 2007, and she thought the service might be helpful to my friend's company. The company's CEO agreed, and the company went ahead and told their sales staffers to read up and learn all they could about using Twitter effectively.

The sales department got some good help from the marketing director—she was a real smart cookie. To roll out the Twitter sales campaign, she ran a contest: once an hour, she posted a holiday-related trivia question (the campaign came out in December). To win, you had to be one of the first three replies with the correct answer. The prize was credit a for one-year contract for free web selling services from my friend's company; to receive it, you needed to open an account with the company.

The company considers the contest a success from a customer-accumulation point of view. The company saw its Twitter follower count jump by five thousand subscribers and saw its Internet-page ranking numbers rise, as well.

But the real interesting wrinkle is how the company's sale staff started improving their numbers. By learning how to interact with the swelling number of new potential customers, they were able to close more sales on their Blackberries and iPhones than they ever did through a Rolodex.

Overall, the company saw a 20-percent spike in sales after the Twitter "learning" campaign. But there is a long-term gain as well. Company sales staffers now have a new weapon in their selling arsenal.

Stories like that reveal why sales is dynamic, and why learning new ways to sell is a constant priority to any successful sales professional.

Q-Tip: *How One Tea-Maker Figured Out to Push "Target" Sales*

Here's a good case study from Steaz Tea that shows the importance for all driven sellers—by learning all they can about their key demographic:

Organic tea brand Steaz needed to generate nation-wide awareness and drive Steaz sales at Target stores—and quickly.

The company felt that if it could get moms talking about Steaz, the sales would follow. To initiate the process, it sent roughly thirty sample kits before Thanksgiving and another thirty before Christmas. Steaz offered to provide give-away prizes to bloggers who wanted to make use of them—things like Internet coupons, Twitter parties, and running a lot of Facebook ads.

The company was confident that it could generate fifty thousand coupon downloads and a thousand new fans/followers—and that this would get Target to notice the little tea brand it had just adopted.

The actual results from the sales campaign were tremendous—over 250,000 coupon downloads (with a 20-plus-percent redemption rate), 6,000 blog and social network mentions, and more than 3,000 new fans/followers—all from moms who shop at Target and who loved tea.

Steaz's December sales were double its previous best month ever. And Steaz shelves in Target stores nationwide were emptied.

That's what I mean about learning all you can about your customers.

What Have I Learned?

I saw a good quote in an article about sales that pretty much sums up where I'm coming from in this book: "If your sales results are not what you thought they would be by now, and if you have been selling for months or years with minimal progress, *your frustrations are not your fault.*"

The takeaway is this: It could be the way you were taught to sell is holding you back.

Consequently, I've learned that selling is a life skill, and like any life skill, it must be approached with honesty, be results oriented, and always, always be focused on the customer.

That hasn't always been the case. For the last few decades, sales training has been all over the map, focused on the manufacturer, the products, the dealership, the manager, the sales process, and everyone but the customer.

That's the most important lesson a sales professional must learn. If, indeed, sales is a life skill, the focus must always be on the customer, not on the product you're selling. That's why I spend so much time learning all I can about my customers and then setting out to meet those wants and needs.

What tools do I use specifically to make that goal achievable? Here are a few I've used over the years.

Always Be Reading. Again, I'm a big advocate for reading. The sales business is always changing, and we need to keep up with those changes. Reading up on the industry is a source of knowledge about change. When you crave knowledge, you learn about changes in business that impact your customers' businesses and then your own. I like to take thirty minutes a day to read something new about sales. That way, I'm always learning.

Learn to set goals—I talked at length about this issue earlier in the book. As a sales pro, your mission is to bring value to your customers. Thus setting goals can add value to your customers in key areas like avoiding cost reductions, or simplifying a product or service issue for your customer.

Who makes the call? Always know who the decision maker is on the customer side of the desk. If you're only calling on one decision maker, if you're unfamiliar with all decision makers, or if you're unaware of each of their concerns, the red light goes on. Pay attention when your contacts move on and are replaced by others. You need to re-establish relationships with the new contact by identifying their key concerns and motivators. Forgetting to do the work to make a new contact loyal will leave you vulnerable to the past loyalties they've established with other suppliers.

Sales works both ways—a sale is being made every time you make a pitch. Either you sell to the customer or he sells you on why he can't buy from you. If you want to be the one closing, you better have a rebuttal for every one of his excuses.

Train your voice—if you sound dull and boring, you are going to put people to sleep. Record your voice and play it back, because you sound different then you think. Ask your friends and family how you sound...get as many opinions as possible. If your voice doesn't sound great, practice until it does.

Case Study: Follow the Money

In the cleaning business, our service is priced on a price-per-square foot basis.

If I am not awarded a particular job, I continue to work the sale to find out why. If, for example, I find out that my competitor offered a better price and I can find that price out, I have a big leg up against the competitor down the road.

How do I find that out? I ask a lot of questions. Believe me, people want to help you to succeed, especially if you ask nicely. People want to help people that they like. Sounds simple, because it is, be nice.

So with that information gained, I can outbid my competitor on the next project, since I have a pretty good idea of where the pricing structure is on the job.

Q-Tip: *Learn How to Give Your Customers Choices*

When giving your customers options, let them have three options.

That's the conclusion of a new brain study that found it was easier for a person to make a decision between three items than it is for two. Here's an example: if you're in the mortgage business, instead of offering a fixed-rate or adjustable-rate loan, add a balloon note to the mix. The study found that buyers were more apt to sign on the bottom line given three choices.

The takeaway: learn to use "threes" and you'll close more deals.

Getting the Most from Your Individualized Sales Training Program

The heart of any formal sales learning infrastructure is a good sales training program. I know, we've all been through them, and many of them are as worthwhile as a lawn mower at the North Pole.

If done right, sales training programs can really help you learn how to hone and sharpen your sales skills. But from what I've experienced, the programs that work best are the ones that set the stage for delivering the best results.

I've taken enough sales training sessions over the years to know what works and what doesn't. So let's cut the wheat from the chaff and examine some sales training fundamentals that can make any "back to school" sales training campaign worth your while.

Good sales training programs must…

- **Have management buy-in:** You send the wrong message when management doesn't take sales training seriously—or not at all. Ideally, the program should be so clear, crisp, and compelling that management can use it to run meetings, solve problems, and for other day-to-day situations.

- **Have measurable results:** You need to have a sales training program that is accountable to the organization. Are your sales staffers closing more deals? Is your company making more money? These are some of the questions that need to be asked.

- **Be brief:** Salespeople are busy and won't connect with a sales training program that goes on and on. In fact, studies show that most training programs fail today just because the segments are too long and lose the attention of the trainees. The lesson here is to keep the sessions concise and emphasize things like interactive engagement and testing. You need to hold your sales staff's interest—and keeping things short will help in that regard.

- **Have a reward element:** Sales training sessions should not only be brief and measurable, they should reward participants. Once again, studies show that concise training sessions done at regular intervals over extended periods of time will create increased levels of sales production. But programs that don't recognize progress and results often fail.

Whether it's an incentive program or a bonus deal for actualizing results, a reward mechanism should be part of any sales training program.

- **Bring everyone in—not just new salespeople**: From what I've seen, most organizations put all their attention and training dollars on the new hires and forget to continue to train the most stable in the organization. Effective sales training programs should focus 80 percent of the training content, time, and energy on the proven salespeople in the organization.

- **Be pervasive:** Sales training should be made part of your company's culture and eventually be melded into everyday activities. For example, each staff meeting should include a training element (that could be a tip, or some fresh insight into a potential customer). The key is this: always be training, even if it's not done formally.

These are the "tried-and-true" keys to a successful training initiative. But feel free to experiment and use what works. Each sales training program has its own pulse and its own dynamic. Find out what works for you and make it a long-term component to your sales organization.

Case Study: Learning to Adapt

Here's a good case study on adapting to real-world sales issues.

The national sales manager for a large insurance company needed a very specific training issue regarding the firm's large, widely dispersed contingent of wholesalers.

After spending time on the road with several members of this sales force, the manager grew concerned that many sales staffers seemed to lack adequate knowledge of the complex variable-insurance products they were representing, and as a result could not effectively respond to questions from financial advisors and brokers. Clearly this had an impact on their effectiveness.

The company determined that it needed a two-pronged training program for the sales force—one that would explore both the complex technical aspects of the product line and ways to apply their knowledge in sales situations.

Because the sales force consisted of seasoned financial professionals, it could create a training program with an advanced approach—emphasizing the complexities of these products and how to sell them, without spending time on basic financial concepts. Employing a variety of adult-learning concepts would help to ensure learning and retention of this detail-oriented curriculum.

But the national sales manager insisted that the sales force be able to remain productive—that is, keep on selling—throughout the training period. This requirement, and the fact that the wholesalers typically are on the road four days a week, made traditional centralized training unacceptable.

This company needed a distance-learning solution to solve these issues. By combining interactive CD-ROMs, web-based exercises, and open-book learning, it could create a course of study that could be completed by the firm's wholesalers wherever they happened to be—whether at their home office or on the road.

Thus the firm was able to keep its entire sales force out in the field while this training took place. This project required neither down time nor additional travel. Individuals could take part in the CD-ROM, scavenger hunt, and web-based exercises at any time, making it practical for new members of the firm's sales force. The small-group discussions could be scheduled once several of these new participants had completed the program.

By adapting to the realities of its core business, the insurance company could keep training sessions going—even as its sales staff was away from the office.

Q-Tip: *Highlight Your Sales Reading*

I want to end this chapter with a tip I've used to get the most from my sales learning—use a pen to highlight key passages in a book—or a "bold" font if you're reading it online.

When you do so, make sure to capture the things that will make a difference for you. Also, go ahead and write notes to yourself in the margins (or make notes online). I don't know about you, but I tend to remember things after I've written them down or highlighted them.

Do This	Not That
Do . . . learn how to study your customers. The more you know about their likes and dislikes, the more deals you'll close.	*Don't . . . assume that you know your customer's thinking unless you've made a focused effort to know their decision-making tendencies. People will surprise you—so learning more about them can reduce those surprises.*
Do . . . make an effort to revisit your sales training program. Training is a great way to learn new strategies and techniques. But that only applies to sales training programs that work for you.	*Don't . . . make your sales training programs long, drawn-out affairs. Sales pros respond to crisp, concise, and compelling training sessions where there is a lot of interaction between the teacher and the students.*
Do . . . read as much as possible. Spend thirty minutes a day reading about something you didn't know about your industry or about the selling business.	*Don't . . . read and forget. Always make notes and highlight key passages. They tend to stick longer with you when you make an effort to note the good stuff (and you'll also forget the bad stuff).*

Chapter Summary

· ·

- Learning is dynamic and ongoing. The best programs are the ones that incorporate lessons learned into everyday sales challenges.

- Learning is what is unique. There's nothing wrong with engaging in a little "trial and error" to find out what works best for you.

- Learning should be fun. Going back to school can sound like a drag. But know this: the more you learn, the more deals you'll close, and the more money you'll make. That sounds like a lot of fun to me.

JUMP-START STEP #4:

Branding: Who Are You?

When I think of the great business brands, I start with Coca-Cola.

It's no accident that Coca-Cola is the king of brands—and the subject of numerous case studies and white papers on successful branding techniques. Studies show that Coke's brand name is known by 90 percent of the world's population.

That's about four hundred million people, from Boston to Brisbane. While there's no shortage of evidence of its image-building success, the beverage giant's branding strategy can be especially found in its current social networking campaign. The Coca-Cola web page is highly interactive; a big component of its strategy is steering people to have a "relationship" with Coke—to take a stake in its growth and success.

It's a good case study on how even a regular sales pro can leverage his or her customer to build a brand—here's a quick look how the Coke brands works in the Information Age:

Get customers involved: For starters, Coca-Cola has taken the unusual step of user-created content on its Facebook site. That's quite a risk for a big, global company to take—you don't really know the quality of the content you're going to get from outsiders. But that's the beauty of Coke's branding style, and sales professional should take note of it. At Coke, the consumer is just as much a stakeholder in the company's message as Coca-Cola is. That's a risky proposition for Coca-Cola, but one that really demonstrates their interest in getting fans involved with the brand. And it works.

Creative use of photos: Coca-Cola also makes great use of "fan photos" showing customers using and enjoying Coke products—and then posting those photos on the website. A big component of the photo section of the site is the high number of Coke fans showing off their Coke collectables. In some cases, they're not even drinking the product as much as showing off their Coke beach towels or illuminated wall clocks. When you can get your customer base to bolster your reputation as a global marketing icon, you've really got a great brand.

Reward your "fan base": Here's something that most companies wouldn't do—have some of its customers build its Facebook page. But that's all part of the Coke image campaign. The Facebook site was first launched by two fans that were self-professed "ambassadors" for Coke. Coca-Cola marketing staffers discovered the page, and rather than trying to buy it or create another "official" page, they rewarded the two fans and worked with them to continue building the page and representing the brand. By giving them the keys to the site rather than brushing them off, Coca-Cola has built a huge reservoir of goodwill and given its existing fan base a chance to grow even larger—and with even greater enthusiasm.

Like Coca-Cola, I have my own brand that works for me.

I've been in the cleaning business since college, and I long ago decided that when I would go out on a sales call, I would wear a suit and tie. Whenever I'm on the job, or in my office, I wanted everyone around me to understand my commitment to my brand. My thinking was this: wherever I was, either with clients or employees, people should understand the importance of presenting a professional appearance.

Dressing up—or dressing down—has long been part of the corporate branding mission. IBM developed its somewhat stuffy, by-the-numbers corporate reputation after its squeaky-clean corporate image—personified by its army of employees who wore white shirts, ties, and dark suits.

The "IBM Way" was manifested by its button-down founder, Robert Watson, who never appeared in public without his trademark suit and tie.

Conversely, Apple developed its cool, laid-back image in large part to the wardrobe and demeanor of its founder, Steve Jobs, hair blow-dried, and perennially clad in blue jeans and a black turtleneck sweater.

Q-Tip: *The Coca-Cola Way*

Coca-Cola has an estimated brand equity value of over $67 billion, making Coke the number one brand in the world. Amazing for a company that sells sugar and water in a can.

Here are the global brand's keys to its professional brand:

- Differentiate yourself from others in similar fields.

- Position yourself clearly in the minds of others.

- Focus your message and your mission.

- Project credibility.

- Develop loyalty.

- Make emotional, visceral connections.

What Is Branding?

It's my opinion that branding is all about perception.

You look at police and firefighters—they wear uniforms to brand themselves. A firefighter in full gear sends a powerful message of toughness and protection—a great brand for a firefighter to project.

Similarly, when I see a salesman in a golf shirt, I know he's going for his own style—an informal approach—like he's just one of the guys.

It's not just about what shirt you wear. In the cleaning business, perception is a huge element in branding. In our business, neatness is as important as cleaning – it creates the right first impression—it is vital that in every building, in every office, on every night we straighten every chair behind every desk and leave a perfect first impression. Attention to detail is part of a salesman's brand-building campaign, too.

I learned the value of good branding at a young age. When I was twenty-two years old and fresh out of Penn State, I got a job in the housekeeping department in an Albany, New York, hotel. The housekeeping manager used to walk around with us on our room tours. He'd bring a tape recorder and would habitually make negative comments on the conditions of the rooms.

But I was young and confident and suggested something different—I would man the clipboard and the tape recorder. My manager was glad to give up the responsibility and I took the job. My main goal was to be more positive in my comments. Within weeks, we were getting better feedback from hotel management on our work.

In effect, I was "branding" our housekeeping staff as a positive operation instead of a negative one.

I've never forgotten that experience and hopefully never will. Your brand, like your reputation, just has to be a priority for sales professionals.

....

Quotable: Branding—the Outlaw Way
Watch your thoughts; they become words.
Watch your words; they become actions.
Watch your actions; they become habits.
Watch your habits; they become character.
Watch your character; it becomes your destiny.

—FRANK OUTLAW

....

Merging Branding and Sales (the Apple Effect)
For sales professionals, branding is a very personal affair.

How so? In reality, branding is your name, your persona, and your reputation. More importantly, like Coke has shown, it's what you see inside your self—and what your customer sees in you.

Consider McDonalds, Mercedes-Benz, or Hershey's Chocolate. They all have great branding. Their branding identifies their product and its perceived value. Hallmark Greeting Cards, for example, built a greeting-card empire on top of the simple, elegant, and highly successful phrase "when you care enough to send the very best." Branding is who you are in the minds of your customers. Too many salespeople focus only on closing sales. They go through all the steps to the sale, from asking questions to closing, but never seek to separate themselves from the competitive pack.

But there is a way for salespeople to do that, and one company in particular shows the way. I mentioned Apple and its CEO, Steve Jobs, a few paragraphs ago. Truly, Apple is one of the greatest branding stories ever—and its lessons learned should be required reading for any sales professional looking to build his or her own brand.

Let's take a look.

In large part, Apple hones its brand by reaching out and breaking boundaries that have reined in their competitors. For twenty-five years or so, Apple only sold computers, but even then the company touted its laptops and desktop computers and accompanying software as "different" than the ones being built by competitors like IBM, Hewlett-Packard, and Microsoft.

Jobs famously returned to Apple in 1997, when the company was on its heels and shedding both customers and its hard-earned reputation as a creative, innovative company. His message was a simple one—rebuild the Apple brand. "We need to reintroduce Apple to those who have forgotten what we stand for, and introduce Apple to everyone else," he said at the time. "I want everyone to know what drives this company, and I want to set the stage for the mind-blowing products we'll start introducing next year."

Jobs' plan was to tell Apple customers—and potential customers—what Apple was all about; i.e. creating amazing products that consumers found both "cool," countercultural, and productive. Before long, Jobs' passion for creativity, design, style, elegance, and simplicity started to find its way into a new line of products, like the iPod, the iPhone, and the iPad. Consumers got a huge kick out of being in on the joke. Apple consumers were radicals, pirates, rule breakers—all the things they otherwise couldn't be in real life.

That was the simple but compelling idea behind the Apple brand—more John Lennon than John Wayne, more Captain Jack Sparrow than Captain America.

Thus the new tagline that fueled the new culture at Apple under Jobs— "Think Different."

As I said, Jobs & Co. used that brand to compete across several highly competitive markets. Apple is using iPod, iPad, iTunes, and the iPhone to reinforce and reinvigorate the Apple-brand personality. At the same time, these product initiatives are growing a highly relevant, appealing brand image in the minds of consumer segments that Apple has not previously reached.

So far, Apples' branding strategy is fueling powerful results. For example, Apple reports that half of all computer sales through its retail channel are to people new to Macintosh, the company's sales and margins have been growing strongly in the first decade of the new millennium, and Apple has achieved several "best ever" quarterly financial results during the past couple of years.

....

Quotable: Make Yourself Noticeable—or Disappear
If you're not appearing, you're disappearing.

—LEGENDARY JAZZ MUSICIAN ART BLAKEY

....

Creating Your Sales Persona

How can a sales professional take a cue from Apple and build his or her own brand identity?

Start by thinking you can do it. Branding should be as equally important to small sales professionals as it is to big multinational corporations like Apple. Unfortunately for them, salespeople often fail to understand that branding can be crucial to their success, and they tend to overlook the importance of branding. In fact, it may be even more crucial to salespeople than large corporations. It ensures a professional look, and enhances confidence in the minds of customers of your ability to provide what you promise. Branding ensures a consistent look—from your business cards, logos, and stationary, to your website.

That's why, for salespeople, branding must be unique and easily recognizable. It is through the brand that potential customers know you. Ensure consistency across the elements of your brand identity, such as logo, business cards, company signage, etc. Try to be personal, to ensure that you do not use very common elements. Consistency, in all your marketing elements, even on Facebook, on Twitter, and via your e-mails, is essential for a professional look, to ensure high visibility and memory retention.

Remember, too, that in sales (*especially in sales*) consumers react emotionally to brands. Buying decisions are made on the basis of emotions and then rationalized. Consequently, branding in the sales market has to build a distinction and differentiation in the consumer's mind and appeal to his/her emotions and lifestyle.

So where do you start in your own personal sales branding campaign? Begin by asking yourself, "what, specifically, do I bring to the table?"

I know—there isn't a salesman or woman alive who doesn't cover all the bases (or thinks they do) and strive to give their customer their best effort. Perhaps a better question to ask is this: "What CAN I bring to the sale?" Think creatively here, beyond the tired, cliché-ridden, "service-with-a-smile" syndrome. Build a personal brand that emphasizes your best qualities—dependability, persuasion, a sense of humor, and (especially) trust can be real brand-building cornerstones.

Trust is particularly issue with me. We all know the story of Tiger Woods, who was caught in numerous affairs with a bevy of women—ultimately his marriage collapsed and he lost tens of millions of dollars in advertising sponsorships.

There was an article on Yahoo.com shortly after the incident called "Woods' Financial Losses May Be Short-Lived." In it, Woods himself is quoted as saying that he could "prove that I am a worthy investment."

But it was another quote that really got my attention. It was from an analyst at a market research group who said "all it's going to take [for Tiger to rebuild his image] is for Tiger to play well, and his value as a spokesperson for a product not only goes right back where it was…but even may increase."

Maybe…and maybe not. What we know for sure is that Tiger Woods committed an unpardonable sin when it comes to branding—he lost the trust of the public. All the positive tenets that Tiger brought to the table—things like commitment, discipline, high energy, focus under pressure—went by the wayside when he was caught cheating on his wife.

Make no mistake: Tiger Woods didn't lose $100 million in sponsorships because he started losing golf tournaments. He lost them because he lost the trust of the public. His brand had become tarnished, perhaps for the long haul, perhaps forever.

That's a good story from a sales perspective. Tiger Woods is a one-man brand—he essentially sells himself and that's it. When he tarnished his reputation, he hurt himself and severely damaged his brand.

And once you sever the brand from your personal reputation, it's tough to get it back.

Tiger Woods lost his customers because his behavior was no longer consistent with what it was that he sold. His behavior was inconsistent with his brand. The takeaway for salespeople is this: always remember that when we sell, we sell ourselves. "We" are our own brands, and when we hurt those brands, we wind up hurting our professional reputations—and will likely lose a lot of sales in the process.

It's a distinction that Apple made a long time ago, and one that Tiger Woods made as he burst onto the global stage. The thing is, Steve Jobs never forgot it and Tiger Woods did.

Building and protecting a good brand has to be a priority for anyone looking to succeed in sales today.

....

Quotable: **Keys to Branding Success: Listen to Your Customer**
The more you engage with customers the clearer things become and the easier it is to determine what you should be doing.

—JOHN RUSSELL, PRESIDENT, HARLEY-DAVIDSON

....

Using Social Media to Build Your Brand

A great way to create your own personal sales brand is to use that great business equalizer—technology. That's the quickest and most pervasive way I know how to make an impression—and ultimately help you close more sales.

If you can manage to master social networking, you'll be away ahead of your competition.

That's because most companies are doing a poor job of using social networks, such as Facebook and Twitter, to engage their customers and employees. According to a recent study by the research firm Yankee Group, 70 percent of consumers want to interact with businesses via social media, but only 30 percent of companies are equipped to handle it.

That study shows that most customers and employees would rather use social media for business communications, but that one-third of enterprises either lack formal social networking polices, don't allow their employees to use social networks at work, or are unaware of their company's participation in social media.

By failing to integrate social networks into regular business communications, sales professionals at such companies are missing a golden opportunity to engage their customers and enhance worker productivity.

"Social media is changing the way businesses, customers, and employees interact, and this creates significant opportunities for contact centers and the enterprise as a whole to leverage the integration of these tools into business processes," said Yankee-group research analyst Zeus Kerravala in a statement.

Other study findings show the importance of a strong social media presence for business:

- Fifty percent of survey respondents use social networks daily, or several times a day.

- Social media boosts devotion: almost 60 percent of customers say that business outreach via social networks would improve their loyalty to a company.

- Enterprises should monitor social networks for consumer feedback, customers say.

- Employees love social media. Nearly 70 percent of workers want better tools to manage social networks for business. Example: they want the ability to launch a web conference and invite people from their social and work networks.

How can we, as salespeople, use social networking to leverage this "golden opportunity"?

I've got a few ideas…and they all involve what I've been talking about in this chapter—selling yourself.

- **Be aware of who you are online.** The Internet truly gives and takes away. For the latter part, always be aware of what the "online you" looks like. If there are any photos of you doing anything unprofessional on the Internet, or there are message boards with inappropriate comments, get rid of them. Anything that reflects poorly on you negatively impacts your brand. Just ask Tiger Woods.

- **Have a great bio or website.** Build a nice website, or a bio on a social networking site. Include a nice photo of you smiling, some testimonials from good customers, and a good cover letter or mission statement stating what you bring to the table from a sales point of view. Post any links to companies you've done business with—they show you have a solid track record of success.

- **Use LinkedIn**—especially the groups. Even if you don't do anything in them, they are badges of honor. Plus, it's a great way to meet some new contacts.

- **Use Twitter.** Yes, it feels strange at first, but it's a quick, surefire way to communicate with clients and potential clients. Even at 140 characters or less, Twitter can help send a big message to clients. When you use Twitter, try to follow experts in your industry—that will help you stay on the forefront of what's selling and what isn't.

- **Know how customers are using social networking.** If you want to know your customer, see what he or she is writing on LinkedIn, on a personal blog, or on a Twitter page. That will tell you what matters to them most, and that can provide some great clues on how to sell to them.

A Personal Branding Checklist
Like anything else in life, your personal branding mission is a dynamic, ever-changing one. As you roll on with your brand building, you'll add new material (like a blog, or a new testimonial from a client).

That said, there are some tools you'll need in order to build and maintain your sales-branding campaign. So, for a quick primer on affordably building brand equity, here is a checklist loaded with branding goals and tips. Carry it around with you; tape it to your fridge—wherever you have easy access to it. If you make it a point to cross off every item on your checklist, by the time you're done, you'll have created the kind of brand that really awakens the sales monster inside of you.

- Become an industry expert. Any brand is enhanced by an industry expert. People like to buy experts, so make it a goal to know your industry cold.

- Learn from the best. Study the branding techniques perfected by the Apples and Coca-Colas of the world. Aim to read at least one case study per week.

- Develop a mission statement. What is your primary goal in rebuilding your sales image? How are you going to get there? Start writing and keep at it until you have your mission statement perfect. Aim for one page or less (keep it simple).

- Create a customized logo and insert it in every one of your collateral messages, including advertising, letterhead, signage, business cards, and website.

- Create a website. Only about half of all salespeople have a website, which might give you a competitive edge over others who don't have one. Keep it current and update it every two years. Insert your logo as a favicon, which is short for "favorites icon", also known as a website icon or a shortcut icon. In this way, it will show up in the search line on users' computers. It will add sophistication to your online image much like bigger companies.

- If you're in sales for a small company, own your keyword names—both your name and that of your company's. If your company is named after you, that's even better. How many quality references does the web have about you?

- Stay current on social media, including LinkedIn, Twitter, and Facebook.

- Tell a great story. People like to buy from salespeople with good stories to tell.

- Be a media maven. Offer your expertise to reporters who cover your industry, and don't forget trade magazines. Don't be discouraged if a reporter doesn't call you. Be patient.

- Create press releases for the media and post them on your website on a "Press" or "Media" page.

- Be a joiner. Be present at as many relevant events in your community as possible.

- Be a joiner, part II: Budget permitting, join your chamber of commerce and industry associations.

- Study search engine optimization (SEO) techniques so customers can easily find you and discover information about your abilities and expertise.

- Always demonstrate that you want to make sales but you don't need them.

- Keep on trying whenever you fail. Every experience is a learning experience.

Q-Tip: *What Customers Want*

Studies show that customers make their buying decisions primarily on their interactions with and influences from you—not price or customer service. That makes building a good personal brand more important than ever.

Here's a breakdown of what customers want:

* What customers perceive about you, your employees, and spokespersons—52 percent

* Image of your company—15 percent

* Quality of product or service utility—13 percent

* Convenience –12 percent

* Price—8 percent

Do This	Not That
Do . . . read up on the branding habits of the great marketing companies like Apple and Coca-Cola. Even though they're big companies, their best ideas are applicable anywhere.	*Don't . . . assume that a brand is strictly about marketing. A successful brand is personal—it gives people a good reason to not only do business with you, but want to keep doing business with you.*
Do . . . make an effort to include technology—especially social networking tools—in your branding campaign.	*Don't . . . assume that you know everything about your online identity. What your online history says about you goes a long way in shaping your brand. Control your online image—and control your brand.*
Do . . . use the checklist listed in the chapter to help build your brand. Add other good ideas to the list as they pop up.	*Don't . . . drop the list or give it "afterthought" status. Know that if you check every item off that list, you're going to be a much better producer.*

Chapter Summary

. . . .

- Your brand dictates how people feel about buying from you.

- A good brand not only energizes you, it also energizes your customers *to want to do business with you.*

- Leverage technology. Get on Facebook. Build a web page. Tweet to customers. We're in the Information Age now—your online image is a huge part of your branding campaign.

JUMP-START STEP 5:

Going ALL In!!

Often the difference between a successful man and a failure is not one's better abilities or ideas, but the courage that one has to bet on his ideas, to take a calculated risk, and to act.

— *MAXWELL MALTZ*

When W. C. Fields famously said, "never give a sucker an even break," some people gleaned more from the line than others did.

Sure, the average American who heard the line shook his head, chuckled, and went on with his life.

But some people didn't. Instead, they took the line and embraced it, like a twelve-year-old clinging to Lebron James' autograph or a high school senior clutching her acceptance letter to Harvard. These people—many of them salespeople—likely won't absorb the Fields quote as simply a well-spun, humorous line from a comedy legend. No, they grasped the line like a man sinking at sea grabs a life preserver.

To them, the line "never give a sucker an even break" is a mantra for the way they live their lives in sales. These are the risk takers and rule breakers that look at economic opportunity differently than everyone else; the people who main-line risk for a living; who sit down for hours, sometimes even days, on end and use their persuasive gifts and well-honed study of human nature to make a good living in the world's toughest but most rewarding profession—sales. Such risk takers know only too well that, like a championship poker player, if you wade into a trading pit or sit down at a poker table and can't identify the "sucker," chances are it's you.

Thus the resonance of the W. C. Fields line—and the foundation of this chapter about risk and reward.

My point? Scratch a sales monster—find a risk taker.

Call me crazy, but combining the top poker strategies and tips with a sales monster mindset is a natural. Masters of both professions know that you can learn the basics of poker and sales in about five minutes and then spend the whole rest of your life trying to understand the nuances. Indeed, poker players and sales professionals who have been at it for twenty or thirty years say they still learn something new every day.

From a risk and opportunity standpoint, poker and sales originate from the same gene pool. Both are endeavors with incomplete and uncertain economic consequences. Both involve vast amounts of information that are both unknowable and uncontrollable.

As Jesse May, legendary poker player and author of the book *Shut Up and Deal*, once said, "Poker is a combination of luck and skill. People think mastering the skill part is hard, but they're wrong. The trick to poker is mastering the luck." That, by no coincidence, is the mindset in sales calls from New York to Tokyo.

Tilting the odds in your favor is another big factor in both vocations. While it's tough to break out a crystal ball and predict how things will shake out around a poker table or on a big sales call, both poker and sales enable you to conduct enough analysis so that the probabilities are in your favor when you decide to act. Furthermore, while the skill sets for both are the same—each places a huge emphasis on risk assessment and quick decision making, with a dash of behavioral psychology tossed into the mix—having the patience of a saint doesn't hurt, either.

An innate understanding of human nature—an understanding that is hard-wired into one's psyche—is also common to poker players and salespeople. Let's face it—sales professionals screw up all of the time. A phone call from a good idea is returned too late; a sales call goes awry when the salesman doesn't understand the client's business. A salesperson over-promises—and then under-delivers.

Similarly, the average poker player makes equally terrible choices at the poker table, either from a heightened sense of greed or a heightened sense of fear (depending on how the game is going). In both cases, people don't make their decisions on a probability basis (a must in both poker and in sales), and they almost always make bad decisions based on emotion.

While the themes mentioned above are the key comparisons between poker and sales, they are not the only ones. Here are some other similarities between poker and sales:

- **Born to Gamble:** Sales monsters and poker player are gamblers, risking time and money to make more money—with a shot of adrenaline thrown into the mix.

- **The "Tell" Test:** Characteristics of salespeople and poker players are also easy to spot: some poker players guard their chips and only bet on sure hands. They don't like to risk too much, and when they bet, most other players will fold. They are similar to sales pros who bide their time for a "golden client" that may never arrive. In poker and in sales, conservative players don't lose much and they don't usually win much.

- **The Vision Thing:** Good poker players, like good salespeople, see clear financial opportunities that others just don't see.

- **Poker Face:** Process management comes into play. Poker players say you can tell a lot about a player by how he keeps his chips organized. Some players' chips are arranged both for order and for function—making it easy to check on how good or bad they're doing at a glance. The chips may also be arranged in piles ready to bet or fold. They're there to make money, play the odds, and not so much to socialize. Other players reveal unorganized piles of chips. The chips are just there, probably the most insignificant part of why the player is in the game. These players are usually there to make contact with people.

- **The "Who Knows?" Factor:** Average sales professionals and poker player see their "games" as having uncertain outcomes. Good players, though, know how to leverage "uncertainty" to their advantage.

There's no question in my mind that the best risk takers are the ones who leave the table—or the sales call—with money in their hands. It's a good case study for all of us in the sales game—think like a champion poker player and become the sales monster I want you to be.

Q-Tip: *Taking Risk Is All About Having Confidence*

Something struck me while watching an old show on ESPN Classic television a while back. It was a profile on baseball legend Pete Rose. In one segment, the reporters were talking to Rose while he took batting practice. One questioner, noting that Rose needed ninety-seven hits to pass Hall-of-Famer Ty Cobb as the all-time baseball hitting champion, he then asked Rose how many at bats would it take to get the ninety-seven hits he needed.

"Ninety-seven," Rose answered, slapping another line drive into the outfield.

"Ninety-seven?" replied the shocked reporter. "Why, that means a 1,000 batting average—ninety-seven hits in ninety-seven at bats. Nobody could do that."

Rose stopped hitting and wiped the sweat off his forehead. "Look, I'm in the confidence business," he said to the reporter. "I go up to the plate each time confident I'm going to get a hit. No exceptions."

It was a lesson in confidence that made a deep impression on me. Sales is a confidence business, too. Maybe the ultimate confidence business. Some salespeople lose sight of that and, in the process, lose confidence in themselves as well.

Plus, it reminds me of my favorite mantra: "Winners expect to win." Every time.

Avoid Your "Comfort Zone"

How do you manage risk; i.e. evaluate opportunities, act on those opportunities, and take the chances you need to take to close deal after deal?

Like the poker player analogy, it's all about taking measured, calculated risk. Actually, taking risks is the easy part. There's an old American proverb that says, "you can't steal second base with your foot on first." Anyone in sales who's lost a deal to a more aggressive competitor can attest to that.

I like that line—it reminds me that in sales, you really have to adapt your personality to close the deal. And that means taking some risks.

If you are going to reinvent yourself as a sales monster, you can't do that without stepping outside of what psychiatrists call your "comfort zone." That's why in sales, it's key that you know who you are, what your limits might be, and how to bypass your boundaries so you can unleash that sales monster inside of you.

Outside of one of those championship poker players, nobody knows about risk and reward better than your best sales professional.

Who would know better? These tigers prowl the sales jungle in the first place because they have total confidence that in sales, they can control their own destiny. Hey, when you're essentially your own boss, you don't sit in the grandstand and wait for success to drop into your hands. These guys and girls aren't bystanders, they're gladiators. They know the rewards (big, fat paydays) and they understand the risks (termination or losing a big sale).

I recall watching the Masters Championship—the year Phil Mickelson won golf's biggest championship after hitting a two-hundred-yard shot from the rough between two trees, five feet from the cup. It was a shot few of his rivals would have attempted. When Mickelson was asked the difference between a good and great shot, he smiled knowingly and simply said, "A great shot is when you pull it off. A smart shot is when you don't have the guts to try it." That's an interesting line, one to definitely mull over if you're in sales.

To hit that remarkable shot, Mickelson had to do what we in sales must do every day if we're going to close sales—get out of our comfort zones.

I'm not advocating taking reckless moves. Sometimes playing the percentages is the way to go. All I'm saying is that if you play things close to the vest 100 percent of the time, you won't meet your goals, or your company's sales goals, for that matter. You start playing defensive and one of your competitors who is taking good, calculated risks will eat your lunch.

In my line of work, I see this happen all the time. Sales professionals who win have a few things in common: they have total confidence in themselves and are 100-percent committed to their own success. Above that, they will take risks—just like Phil Mickelson or a good poker player would. When you see that opening, you've got to take it. As the old saying goes, "he who hesitates loses out." Or, as my mother used to say when she called us to dinner, "there are two types of people in the world—the quick and the hungry."

The "hungry," as I define it, are the salespeople who refuse to get out of their comfort zones. They have the same routines, depend on the same clients, and basically stop challenging themselves. In the sales game, if you stop challenging yourself, you stop—period.

The "quick" are the sales professionals who define their success by the opportunities they see, and by the risks they take to close deals when those opportunities present themselves. These championship performers excel at taking risks like cold-calling, knocking closing situations out of the park, embracing new products, and taking the road less traveled when recruiting and managing their field offices.

These top performers know that to succeed—to really succeed—you have to get out of the "same old, same old."

Q-Tip: *How Can You Recognize a "Comfort Zone"*

Sales professionals don't do it deliberately, but many are good at creating comfort zones nonetheless. It can happen in the most innocuous ways: calling on the same types of customers, selling the same type of product or service, or relying too much on a few customers/contacts/decision makers who may not be around next year.

If you fall into a pattern of applying the same tactics and strategies to your sales career, it's time to take stock. Ask your peers, talk to your customers, speak to your manager. Ask them what you can do to shake things up and get out of your safety zone.

Getting Out of Your Comfort Zone

How can you rid yourself of those shackles that come part and parcel with safety zones?

The first thing *not* to do is beat yourself up over the fact that you live in your comfort zone. Believe me, you're not alone—a lot of people do that. One explanation I've heard about comfort zones for sales professionals is that they're the job-related expression of human nature.

Obviously, we like to stick close to the people, actions, and places that are familiar to us. Anyone who's lived in the same home for twenty years or who's had the same friends for thirty years can legitimately claim that they've found familiarity to be a happy, healthful addition to their lives.

But that mindset doesn't really work in sales. The root of the problem is actually the opposite of the comfort zone—the "discomfort zone." If you're out on a sales call, in a strange city that you had to take an airplane to get to, talking to people you don't know—that's a fair description of a discomfort zone. Unfortunately, it's also a pretty good description of life in general for a salesperson.

Or how about this? You're generally OK in talking to customers who are on a lower rung on the management ladder—say, a production manager. But when you need to climb the ladder and start persuading a chief financial officer or even a chief executive officer, the rise in rank may be something that's out of your comfort zone.

It's an interesting dichotomy. The closer you get to a decision maker, the more the pressure rises. The more the pressure rises, the further out of your comfort zone you're likely to get.

The top producers who accept the pressure—who embrace the pressure—are the ones who routinely flourish outside of their safety zones. Why? Because they are able to apply confidence to the process. And where do they get that confidence? From years and years of experience, trial and error, and knowing what tactics they can use to gain a customer's confidence—to the point where a good relationship is built and the path to "yes" rapidly becomes a direct one.

Don't worry—you can get out of your comfort zone, too. Let's start that process by taking you through a few key actionable steps that will have you regaining your confidence and becoming the kind of sales monster that thrives and excels no matter what "zone" you reside in.

- **Create your own experience**. A big step toward freeing yourself in sales is to practice good habits. In the case of "comfort zones," that can mean placing twenty cold calls to high-level decision makers. Don't worry about selling anything—although if you do, that's a great bonus. Just get used to talking to bigwigs—try to focus on listening and learning from what you hear.

- **Get a mentor**. Try to pair yourself with another producer who's more seasoned and more used to trying new tactics to close sales. Go on sales calls with your mentor, sit in on cold calls, and generally try to soak up as much information as possible. Take notes, practice what you see your mentor do, and get used to getting out of your comfort zone.

- **Educate yourself.** A big part of the reason salespeople fall back into safety zones is because they don't know any better. When it comes to sales, even a little knowledge can go a long, long way. And the more you know, the farther you'll go. So take full advantage of company training sessions, industry associations, online sales-board chat rooms—and even local Chamber of Commerce meetings. The idea is to arm yourself with enough information to where you're fully prepared to make your sales case no matter what the environment.

My promise to you is this: If you adopt the tips and strategies I laid out above, you'll grow out of your comfort zone, and better yet, you'll be fully armed and ready to take the kinds of risks you'll need to unleash that sales monster inside of you.

Taking Smart Risks—By Taking Your Time

Boca Raton, Florida, entrepreneur Robert Reiss has something to teach us all about risk.

Specifically, how to manage it, leverage it, and make risk work time and time again.

Reiss says he owes his success as a business owner to *managing* risk so it fits his specific needs.

Reiss has started sixteen small-business ventures in his career, virtually all of them in high-risk markets—selling flea-market type items whose shelf life may be a short one. "You try lots and lots of things, because you don't know what's going to work," he says.

Reiss jumps in and out of markets on what at first glance appears to be a whim—like when he feels that his fad products stop selling. But Reiss is way smarter than that. What he's really doing is adroitly managing risk.

Or as he puts it, he is "dividing risk up with other people." On most business ventures, Reiss is very calculating in how he applies risk—or if he applies it at all.

In the early 1980s, when the board game Trivial Pursuit was all the rage, Reiss took the idea for a competing board game to two powerful entities—a venture capital friend he knew and TV Guide, which had the brand name to post up against a giant like Trivial Pursuit.

Reiss got all the funding from his venture-capital buddy and signed TV Guide up for its name recognition (the product was called the TV Guide Television Trivia Game. The venture made millions on a small $50,000 investment).

Reiss got rich by playing the risk game like a champion poker player. He identified an opportunity, assembled a team that could leverage that opportunity, then reaped the rewards after spreading the risk around.

That's a good lesson for sales performers. You already have resources—a good management team, a great support staff, (hopefully) a sales network to rely on, and a good service to sell. Like Reiss, sales professionals need to leverage all of their strengths by "spreading the risk around."

The Four Kinds of Sales Personalities

Have you heard about the "Four Kinds of Sales Personalities"? Each one assesses risk on a daily basis, but not always in the same way.

- The Engaging Personality

- The Confident Personality

- The Persuasive Personality

- The Dynamic Personality

Let's take a closer look at each category, including how each applies risk to their sales careers:

- **The Engaging Personality**. The risk strategy for the "engaging personality" is to rely, perhaps overly so, on persuasion and charm. That's OK, everyone likes to be wooed and courted. But the key here is for the engaging-personality type to really listen to the client, know what they want, and then and only then, release the charm offensive.

- **The Confident Personality**. The risk with the "confident personality" is to trust that customers believe you. That means a healthy dose of relationship building. Customers only trust you if they know you. So don't ever bend the truth, make sure you always level with your client, and deliver what you say you'll deliver—and you can gain that trust.

- **The Persuasive Personality**. The risk here is that the persuasive personality relies too much on his or her ability to close—at the expense of other sales needed to set a solid close. Make sure to plan ahead, hit your preparation spots, do your homework, and build those relationships—and the closing will be all that much easier.

- **The Dynamic Personality**. This one is a variation of the "engaging personality." The risks that dynamic personalities take are relying too much on their presentation skills to bail them out of tough sells. Of course, being a great presenter is a key attribute to successful selling, But not at the expense of everything else.

Me? I'm a big believer in taking risks, just calculated ones.

I know that my business is going nowhere without taking risks. The biggest threat to a successful salesperson is the willingness to remain comfortable and reject the small risk that could lead to greater rewards.

I recall the story of Gordon McGovern, who founded premium cookie maker Pepperidge Farm. A few years later, McGovern became chairman of Campbell Soup Company. After his hit with Pepperidge Farms, he didn't rest on his laurels. He quickly produced a line of gourmet soups that opened new markets. Sales soared, and more importantly, McGovern's creative, take-a-risk attitude soon permeated the company.

Q-Tip: *Celtic Pride*

Basketball Champion Bill Russell told the following story and every top producer should hear it. He said, "When I was in the eleventh grade, I was cut from the junior varsity basketball team (really smart coach!). Our varsity coach then approached me and asked me to play on the varsity team. "I just got cut from the JV Team," I said. His answer: "I'm not coaching the JV." The moral of this story? Go with your instincts—you may just be right.

Do This	Not That
Do . . . take risks—just smart, measured risks, based on good research, and only when opportunities present themselves. Think like a poker player, and act accordingly.	*Don't . . . take risk management as an open invitation to take wild, reckless gambles. Be smart, and know when to take risks and when to step back.*
Do . . . get out of your comfort zones, and do that by learning, build mentoring relationships, and practice, practice, practice.	*Don't . . . fall into the trap of limiting your opportunities. Getting out of your comfort zone is all about maximizing opportunities—and jumping in when they surface.*
Do . . . manage risk and reward by spreading the risk around, so it all doesn't fall on your shoulders. With more help, you'll have more success stories.	*Don't . . . sell risk and reward short. Become a champion sales producer by learning all you can about risk management. Read books, watch videos, soak up all the information you can get from other sales masters—then be confident and go out and execute your own risk-management plan.*

Chapter Summary

. . . .

- Good risk managers are like good poker players.

- Get out of your comfort zone.

- Amplify your risk-management techniques by learning all you can about risk and reward—and all you can about your customers.

JUMP-START STEP #6:

Monster Time: Let's Get Some Sales

There are risks and costs to action. But they are far less than the long-range risks of comfortable inaction

—JOHN F. KENNEDY

In a word, closing sales is all about taking action.

Why is one salesperson better than other? Because he or she takes action on all fronts. Think about it. A mediocre salesperson tells. A good salesperson explains. A superior salesperson demonstrates. But a master salesperson inspires the buyers to see the benefits of buying his service as their own.

That salesman *took control* over the customer's sale experience. History is filled with examples of that happening. George Westinghouse, founder of the home appliance company that bore his name, once said that other business leaders in his day knew as much as he did about electricity and natural gas. But he figured out a way to invent devices that transmitted gas and alternating currents at a lower rate.

Others take action in more creative ways. There was a legendary salesman named Steve Miller who had tried for months to get an appointment with a hot prospect. He was about to give up one day, but came up with an ingenious scheme: at the airport one day he bought an insurance policy for his flight and made the elusive prospect his beneficiary. He mailed the policy to his potential client, attaching a note that simply said, "Thinking of you." The prospect called him shortly afterward and gave him the appointment.

Separating Yourself from the Pack

That's the kind of drive and action that separates the champion sellers from the rest of the pack.

Miller knew instinctively that if you want to get some sales, you have to go out and get those sales.

That's exactly what I want to talk about here in Chapter Eight—going out and grabbing those sales by the scruff of the neck. Taking what's yours. Getting after it. Hey, any phrase you want to use—as long as it leads to turning leads into sales.

It's my view that the critical step in garnering more sales is a very simple but often overlooked one—do something every day. That could mean making just one more phone call. Or sending one last e-mail to a new prospect. Or setting aside fifteen minutes per day to do a little extra.

I like the latter approach. My fifteen minutes per day are sacred, and I don't let anyone compromise it. I use that time to generate new leads, to follow up on existing leads, or do something outside my existing business—like read a quick article on sales techniques that work—during those minutes.

One exercise in particular that I practice on a regular basis during those fifteen minutes is to train myself to deal in specifics. After all, your competition—especially the ones who have already figures this out—has specific plans on how to take business away from you. Remember the movie *Wall Street*? There is a scene in the movie where Gordon Gekko tells Bud Fox (played by a young Charlie Sheen) to go read Sun Tzu's *The Art of War*. Late in the film, Fox sites the book as a newfound reason for his confidence and aggressiveness. "If your enemy is superior, evade him," Fox says. "If angry, irritate him. If equally matched, fight; and if not, split and reevaluate."

That scene motivated me so much that I went out and bought the book myself. Sun-Tzu was a warrior after my own heart. He knew that to reach his objectives, he had to know his enemy and then craft a plan to defeat him.

Another infamous quote from that movie comes from Gekko. "The most valuable commodity that I know of is information," he says.

That's why I have a computer-software program that tracks all of my prospects. Each prospect is classified in stages, akin to the development of a piece of fruit. It works like this:

- Initial prospects are our seeds.

- As they progress, our pieces of fruit are in the growing stage.

- When we make a presentation, the fruit is reaching optimal growth.

- When we are confident about closing the sale, that means the fruit is ripe.

Q-Tip: *Know Your Prey: Part I*

In sales, knowing whom to target is critical. Yes, I know this sounds simple, but given the matrix-heavy way organizations are structured today, it's important to find out - by networking, by asking questions, by any means possible - until you know the name of the decision maker. When you get that name, here's a tip: once I have a contact name, I will try dialing AFTER-HOURS. These days, most companies have a spell-by-name directory that should give you a direct dial extension. That trick allows you to bypass the standard firewalls, most likely a receptionist.

Fine-Tuning Your Targeting Campaign

My next move is right out of the sales monster's handbook—fine-tune the perfect pitch. I usually pitch potential clients on the phone.

My best advice here is to make a list of "do's and don'ts" for phone sales success. Part of that success program includes phone etiquette, too. Here's a quick snapshot of the opening lines I use—and you should use, too.

- **Stay away from the usual platitudes.** Don't ask, "How are you doing?" or "So, how's your day?" or "When would be a good time to meet?" These questions waste your prospect's time. Worse, they serve to annoy. Instead, focus on getting to the point, quickly. State why you are calling and why your product or service is going to help your prospect. Point out why you are different from your competition. Make sure to avoid negative comments about your competitors—customers consider that bad form. Instead, concentrate on putting *your* product/service in a positive light.

- **Practice, practice, practice.** Every opera singer needs to practice his or her pitch—and so do you. Make a habit of rehearsing your script, and focus on the positive. What *you* can do to solve *your* clients' problems?

- **Get a mentor involved (or at least a partner).** Role-playing with a mentor is well worth the effort. Whenever I hire a new sales person, I have them call me on the phone and give me a pitch. Every time, I give my "partner" objectives they must overcome. I'll do this repeatedly until the pitch is unique to my new sales staffer. In time, the new hire becomes comfortable overcoming objectives, because in sales you get objectives—lots of them. In the end, it's how you respond to objectives that separates the wheat from the chaff in sales.

- **Think theory, then execution.** Always consider your objectives and your response to those objectives. That'll help when surprises occur on pitch calls—and they always do.

- **Keep it fresh.** Many salespeople I run into rely on the same scripted, robotic speech. Avoid this approach like the plague. When you rely on a scripted dialogue, you tend to state the benefits of your product or service without conviction. Then it's a short trip to becoming complacent about the competition. Keep it fresh—blend in new material and keep the dialogue on a direct but engaging course. Of course, a good sense of humor helps.

- **Tap existing customers.** Your current customers are like gold, from an informational point of view. Ask them some very simple questions: How do you like to be sold? What do you look for in a salesperson? Tell me about your best sales experience? What made it so good?

Prequalify your prospects. This is a great timesaver. There's no question that qualified prospects are great sales opportunities—they have an acknowledged need for your product or service, can pay for that product or service, and are likely to do business with you. If you spend more time finding and vetting likely buyers, you'll save tons of time you'd otherwise be wasting chasing dubious leads down dark financial alleys.

Q-TIP: *Gain Sales Leads Online—Hosting your own online webinar is a great way to gain new sales. You're going to have to promote it, though. Aim to start touting your webinar about six weeks ahead of your target date.*
Some other tips:

- Conduct an e-mail blast to all your existing clients.

- Cleanly place the registration information on your website.

- Get your company to promote the event on its website. Advertise in the local paper, too.

Getting Knockout Referrals

While I'm on the subject of existing customers, know that invariably, they are the best source of referrals. Any sales champion can tell you that the best leads come by way of somebody giving you a good lead. The right referral is already close to qualified and much, much closer to a buying decision. Remember that every referral you make today is a potential referral down the road. Also remember that sales is a personal-relationship business anchored by referrals—they're the life blood of the industry.

But there's an art to getting those referrals, and I'm going to show you how. Job one is to get past the awkwardness of asking your current customers for referrals. I jump that hurdle by asking about their satisfaction level with your service and product. If you get a good response, tell them you'd appreciate any names of people who might also like to know about the benefits of your business. Ask them to be references or to give testimonials.

It's really not that tough—people want to help. In my experience, customers like taking care of their favorite salespeople, just like we appreciate taking care of them.

Here are a few tips on taking full advantage of sales leads that I've put to good use in my career.

- **Move fast.** Studies have demonstrated that "speed-to-call" is the biggest factor in lead conversion in the initial 120 seconds after a lead is generated. The data shows that if you jump on a lead within 60 seconds (by telephone, not literally), conversion rates jump by almost 400 percent. The lesson here is that when you get a good referral, don't sit on it. The numbers clearly show that it's those who pounce quickly who come away with the sale.

- **Follow Up.** Jumping on a good lead is important, so also know that following up on that lead may be just as critical. There is, however, a limit to how many times you follow up. A global study of sales leads found that contacting prospects six times is the optimal way to obtain good conversion rates without annoying your customers or wasting your and your staff's time. The best way to follow up is to

    o   call three times on the first day;

    o   call once on the third day;

    o   call once on the fourth day; and

    o   call one final time on the twelfth day.

The study notes that the sixth call returned a 500-percent improvement over average conversion rates.

- **Tend to your leads.** You've really got to nurture your leads. After all, not every lead is going to sign on the dotted line right away. That's why it's important to keep tabs on leads that aren't ready to play ball. So that by mixing things up. Use the phone, e-mail, texts and tweets, newsletters, personal notes, and follow-up calls in your follow-up campaign. Space things out—customers don't appreciate being overwhelmed. Alleviate that by spoon-feeding your prospect small bites of information. That will improve the chances of your message being received—on the terms you want your lead to receive it.

There's one last tip on reaching out to your customers that I'll leave you with in this section. Make sure you create some fresh, clean, informative marketing materials *using* your existing customers. That will play a big part in a bigger project—creating excitement about your product or service. Remember that everyone likes a winner, they love to hop on a bandwagon.

If your customers feel that your product/service is a winner, they will act as salespeople for you and *your* business. Those are the kinds of sales leads that money just can't buy.

Q-Tip: *Never forget to send the follow-up e-mail thanking your prospect for his or her time.*

Lessons from a Corning Glass Salesman

Let's continue our conversation on active selling, starting with a great story about a Corning Glass salesman who really knew how to sell one of the company's key products—safety glass.

The salesman knew his stuff. Soon, he became the top-selling salesman of safety glass for Corning Glass in North America. At a big sales convention, he was given a cash prize and an award. What's more, audience members pleaded with the salesman: "Please tell us your secret. How is it that you sold so much more than everyone else?"

The Corning Glass guy said it was simple.

"First of all, I got some pieces of safety glass cut into 6" X 6" pieces as samples. Then, I got a ball-peen hammer. Then I walked in on the prospect and say,

'Would you like to see a piece of glass that doesn't shatter?' When the prospect says, 'I don't believe it,' I put the glass on the counter, take my hammer and whack it—watch him protect his eyes—and afterwards he'd say, 'Holy smoke, that's incredible!'

"Then I'd say, 'How much of it would you like?' And I'd pull out my order pad and start writing the order."

The lesson wasn't lost on Corning Glass. The company was so taken with the salesman's approach that it equipped all of their salespeople with ball-peen hammers and sheets of glass and sent them out—and they all sold truckloads.

I love that story. Here's a guy who combined some of the best attributes of a monster salesman—creativity, ingenuity, and tenacity. His approach was so good that the Corning salesman didn't have to close his sales—his product and his approach did it for him.

Q-Tip: *Know Your Prey: Part II*

Every time—and I mean *every* time—prior to going into meet with a new prospect, I take some specific steps.

First, I Google the name of my contact, and I track the contact to a LinkedIn page or some sort of "bio" page. The information I find there is priceless. Maybe my contact went to Penn State (where I went to school, incidentally). Or maybe some other piece of information will present itself—like the name of an old company where I have contacts. I also visit the company website, where I try to find other "in-house" customers that I already know.

It's a little like playing Sherlock Holmes, but the data threads you can follow on the hunt to close a sale can lead you to some pretty big fish, sales-wise.

How To Sell in Tough Economic Times

I didn't want to end our discussion on reaching out to customers without a word on selling in a tough economy.

Times have changed, and not for the better, economically. Unemployment is up, more homes are being foreclosed, and companies are tossing nickels around like manhole covers.

So how do you sell in a rough-and-tumble economy?

Be an optimist. For starters, think positively. I can't think of a bigger waste of time than brooding and pouting about the lackluster business climate. Even if unemployment is at 10 percent or so, that means 90 percent of the workforce is still employed, and that people and companies are still spending money.

Focus not on limits, but on opportunities. Like I said, there's no point dwelling on the negative. Instead, focus on opportunities. People are still buying, but it might not be in the usual ways. That makes it more imperative to talk to your clients, listen to your clients, and find out how their businesses are adjusting in recessionary times. Also, find out exactly what your clients are looking for. Is it quality? Price? Or both?

Experiment with some game-changers. In tough times, it's time to try fresh approaches. Try hosting a seminar if you've never done that before, or start tweeting useful info to clients. Repositioning yourself as an expert in your field could make a huge difference when the economy is soft and selling is hard.

Why not you? Even in lousy economic times, somewhere a salesperson is out there breaking records. Why can't you post your best sales record? Why can't you up your average gross sales figures? Why can't you add new customers? Someone is going to top their old results—it might as well be you.

Q-Tip: *By the Numbers*
Let's do a little statistical work here. It will help demonstrate what else separates sellers from pretenders:

- 65 percent of a sales rep's time is spent NOT selling.

- The top 26 percent of salespeople have the ability to engage their prospects earlier, redirect their prospects backward in the sales process, position themselves as trusted advisers, and differentiate themselves from their competitors.

- Over 30 percent of all salespeople quit or are released within eighteen months.

- It's estimated that 15 percent of all salespeople capture a staggering 70 percent of the business.

- The reason 80 percent of all salespeople fail, or fail to reach their sales objective, is due to a lack of planning."

- Fifty percent of all salespeople give up after the first contact, and 90 percent quit after the fourth attempt, just a step or two away from the sale.

- Approximately 35 percent of all salespeople across every industry struggle with social self-consciousness."

Sales Lead Checklist

Targeted sales leads aren't a luxury—they're a necessity. Review your lead program with the checklist below:

- Are you prepared to send requested information immediately?

- Do you know what to send in response to different types of inquiries?

- Do you have electronic versions for those who want the information by e-mail or by download from your website?

- Do you have adequate supplies of printed materials ready for those who prefer them?

- Do you have the people, systems, and processes in place to get the requested information out the door quickly?

- Are you prepared to capture all inquiries in a database for ongoing nurturing and qualification efforts?

- Do you have the database ready to go?

- Do you have the data-entry people or outside services lined up to get the inquirers into the database?

- Do you have proactive programs in place to contact and qualify your leads?

- Do you have a process in place for distributing qualified leads to sales contacts as they are identified?

- Does your company have a prospect relationship marketing program in place to keep in touch with these longer-term prospects using e-mail, fax, mail, and phone contacts until they are identified as being qualified and ready for sales attention?

- Do you know what messages to send as part of your prospect relationship management program?

- Do you know how often to contact prospects with these messages?

- Do you know what offers to use to get them to further identify their needs and situations so you can determine if they are ready for sales?

- Do you have a program in place to measure and track the results of your various sales-lead generation, cultivation, and sales follow-up programs?

- Can you determine your cost per lead, cost per qualified lead and cost per sale?

- Do you know which lead programs generate the highest returns on investment?

- Do you know which nurturing techniques worked and which didn't?

- Can you prove to management that your lead-generation programs are paying off in increased sales and market share?

Do This	Not That
Do . . . make use of the clock—call potential clients before or after business hours, when they're likely to be more accessible.	*Don't . . . rely on the usual phone call banter. Get right to the point. What are you going to do to help this customer?*
Do . . . jump on fresh referrals. Studies show that the quicker you follow up on a lead, the better the chance you'll net a new customer.	*Don't . . . try to go it alone. Ask your company for help, get some fresh marketing materials out to your client, and join industry associations where you can meet new people.*
Do . . . be as creative as you can. Remember the Corning Glass salesman story. Be creative and be tenacious.	*Don't . . . fret over the economy. Even with unemployment at 10 percent, that means 90 percent of the country is still working—and spending money.*

Chapter Summary

Targeting sales is the bread and butter of the business.

- Practice your sales pitch. Practice it some more.
- Learn the fine art of turning referrals into clients
- Be optimistic. Sales are always out there. Why shouldn't you be the one to get them?

JUMP-START STEP #7:

Customers for Life: Mastering the "Close"

....

Paralyze resistance with persistence

— WOODY HAYES

....

We've covered a lot of ground inside these pages, especially the parts about finding yourself, finding your sales mojo, and finding customers.

Now it's time to pull the lever and close those sales you've been targeting—the "harvesting" part of sales.

That's what we'll do now. I'd like to start by acknowledging that closing sales isn't easy. Hey, finding and grooming clients isn't easy, but closing is the real tough part.

Don't let that distract you. You're going to have some speed bumps and set-backs on your journey to unlocking the sales monster that's inside of you.

That's perfectly OK—it's all part of the sales process.

Let's begin by bringing in a powerful tool that I've been using for years to rack up big sales—the Monster Cheat Sheet:

Monster Cheat Sheet

Client Number		Date Started	
Client Name/ Nickname		Business Affiliations	
Title		Previous Employers	
Company Name/ Address		Status Symbols in Office	
Phone Numbers		Politically Active/Affiliation	
Birthday/Birthplace/ Age		Religious Affiliation and Importance	
Hometown		Community Involvements	
Education		Clubs/Organizations	
High School-Year		Pets? Names	
College-Year/other degrees		Does Individual Smoke?	
Fraternity/Sports/etc		Does Individual Drink? What?	
Military Service		Favorite Restaurants	
Marital Status/ Anniversary		Type of Car	
Spouse's Name/ Education		Spectator Sports interested in/Favorite teams	
Spouse's Hobbies/ Interests		Favorite Vacation Spots	
Children's Names/ Ages		Favorite Topics	
Children's Education		Topics to avoid	
Children's Interests/ Sports/Hobbies		Miscellaneous information	

Figure 9-1

Use This Customer Profile Sheet

Here's the Customer/Prospect Profile Sheet (aka the "Monster Cheat Sheet")
see figure 9-1. Use it to gain at least one new piece of information on each
customer. The better you know your customer, the more topics you'll have to
speak about—and what topics to avoid (that one really comes in handy).

Here are some things to gather:

- Birthdays

- Anniversaries

- Children's graduations

- New cars purchased

- Career milestones

If you treat your customers right, they'll reward you with referrals to their
friends and relatives. If you've done your job well, you'll soon have lots of new
customers—courtesy of your older ones.

The Monster Sheet has been a great help to me, and it can be a great help
for you, too.

After all, any sales professional knows that you can't close every sale. But what
you can do is believe you can get every customer to sign on the bottom line—but
only if you organize your game plan (that's where the Monster Cheat Sheet comes
in) and only if you believe in yourself. After all, there's no point in meeting a client
if you thought it wouldn't result in a sale at some point in time. That would be negative thinking, and negative thinkers don't last long in the sales game.

The way I look at it, I expect there to be some problems. Even more, I welcome them. After all, when it comes to my customers, their problems are my
problems. Often, those problems open up opportunities to build even stronger
relationships with my clients.

There's an old story about Michael Faraday, the Englander who invented the
first electric motor. Before he could finish the job, he wanted the backing and
interest of the British government. He took the motor—a crude prototype—to
Prime Minister William Gladstone, who wasn't impressed.

"What good is it?" asked Gladstone.

Faraday smiled and responded, "Someday, you'll be able to tax it."

I love that story. Imagine seeing a distress situation, and having the presence of mind and the ability to think on your feet, to say exactly what the customer needs to hear.

Now, *that's* good closing.

Keys to Closing

Closing sales is all about knowing your customer and knowing you're confident.

That's not always so simple.

I knew a guy once who was one of those technology-whiz kids that came along in the late 1980s when the personal computer was just about to break out commercially.

He was one of the first salespeople to have a cell phone in his car and, a few years later, was one of the first to have a portable hand-held computer to keep track of his customers. Thus, he was well equipped to handle the mounting demands of managing busy customers from a logistical sense, but not a humanistic sense. "I had all the gizmos and gadgets and that impressed people for a while," he told me once. "Hell, it impressed me, too. In fact, I was so impressed with myself that I totally missed out on the growing part of the sales/client relationship that you're always so hopped up about. It really impacted my ability to close."

He plead guilty as charged—but today he's hopped up on closing sales for good reason: it's how he feeds and shelters his family.

That point aside, this guy had totally bought into this "total customer management" approach making the rounds in the 1990s that emphasized computers and software and cell phones, but had nothing to say about one-to-one, face-to-face contact—the kinds of meetings where you get to know your clients and hear what their problems are.

Look, I knew where my sales associate was coming from. I had also collected all the high-tech tools throughout my sales career. The cell phone, the Blackberry, the Dell laptop that I always took with me to sales seminars and road trips. I was never out of touch with my clients.

But all the technology in the world couldn't help you really keep in touch with your clients, either.

"Don't get me wrong," I told the guy. "I think you can grow your sales business by using faxes and e-mails and cell phones." In fact, I'd reflected from time to time that it was apparent no salesperson would succeed these days without all the toys and tools they used to keep in touch with their clients. "But it's just a key component of your sales business."

That conversation took place years ago, but I remember it like it was yesterday. I believed then, as I believe now, that expanding my business and keeping more of my clients was a lot more than making sure my cell phone was fully charged. Sure, you needed the organized systems and the database to keep track of everything; and you needed the cell phone and the e-mail to stay connected no matter where you were. But I finally figured out that the difference was continuous, special care of my clients, with a good dose of dedication and, yes, persistence to understand what my customers wanted from me so they could thrive—and so I could thrive, too.

For example, one of my customers had to make a presentation to upper management to gain buy-in on a project. My product would only be a small piece of the overall project so I wasn't too involved, but when I realized that my customer had no idea how to make an effective successful PowerPoint presentation to their management, I knew I had to jump in and help—not just with my piece, but his entire presentation.

So I spent a day with him, developing slides, graphs, ROI—the whole nine yards. In my mind, it was just the right thing to do. Better yet, they bought the project. I got my small sale, but what I really got was goodwill from my client—I'm still getting referrals two years later. I was the difference between high tech and high touch.

Q-Tip: *Meeting Client Expectations*
No doubt about it, customers have certain expectations of sales individuals.

Here's a quick list:

- They have knowledge.

- They are professional (well branded).

- They are honest and well mannered.

- They have the customer's best interest at heart.

- They are fair in pricing.

- They are reliable.

- They believe in what they are selling.

Know What Your Customer Wants

There's another good story about an executive recruiter with his own firm.

He'd spent a month or so trying to place this sales woman into a good job but hadn't had much success. She was a great salesperson but the market was tight and they couldn't get any traction.

One day he got a call from a magazine publishing company looking for a regional director of sales. He was so excited he got right off the phone and called his client, and she immediately went off for an interview.

Several hours later the phone rang and the saleswoman was on the other end. It seemed that the magazine publisher produced…ah…adult-rated magazines. "I can't believe you sent me there!" she screamed into the phone.

Of course, the recruiter was appalled and was very apologetic. In time, the saleswoman forgot about it, but she used another recruiter to land a job. The lesson learned, the recruiter discovered, was to always know your clients' wants and needs.

And never surprise them with something they don't want or need.

Q-Tip: *Seven Ways You Can Jump Start Sales*
Everyone seems to have a different strategy to close sales.

The pharmaceutical industry, for example, believes in sales redundancy. That means they target and call on specific customers to get the job done. They also use multiple sales reps to sell the same product. Why? Because certain personalities work well with certain customers—industry sales managers call that the "power of redundancy."

Seven ways that YOU can jump-start your sales:

- *Be consistent. See your customers on a regularly scheduled basis.*

- *Have a purpose for every visit. PLAN your visits.*

- *Ensure your products/service is meeting the ongoing needs of your customer.*

- *Make sure your customer always feels like your most important customer. Never rush your visit, but don't overstay your welcome.*

- *Gain a new piece of information about your customer on each visit. Use the Monster Cheat Sheet!!*

- *Ask your existing customers, How do you like to sell? What would you do as a sales person?*

- *Ask for referrals.*

Also, simply thank your existing customers. If you're in a business where you repeatedly call on the same customers over and over again, like pharmaceutical sales, it's a big help to just say "thanks." Actually, a handwritten "thank you" note is powerful tool to a sales monster. Every salesperson can benefit from taking time to thank existing customers.

Remember the old saying: "It takes years to win a customer and only seconds to lose one."

Traits of a Great Closer

In my experience, good salespeople are experts at the communications side of the game.

They put the time in to get to really know a client—and I mean listening at least 75 percent of the time for months on end, which many are incapable of doing. But by the time they're done, they can tell by the inflection of a voice over the phone or the look in a customer's eye that says, "Let's do business." They know it instinctively because they've done their homework. So they know when it's time to harvest, because the client is spreading all kinds of nonverbal clues around."

Sure, we'd all love our clients to just pick up the phone and pop $30,000 orders. Unfortunately, that doesn't happen very often. That's why you've got to know their moods and nuances. You've got to read them like a book.

How do you know when you're client is ready to do business? No question, it's an art form.

The best closers know just when to pounce. They have that radar that tells them when a client is ripe for the sale. How do they do it? What traits do the great closers have that others in sales don't?

I've come up with a few traits I've studied in the best closers that I've seen.

Great closers know their customers. Give me a closer who doesn't just qualify customers—he or she knows what they want and knows what they need. Good closers are great at asking good, smart questions—getting customers to reveal more and more of themselves with each answer. And salespeople who get good answers are salespeople who close.

Great closers bring "smarts" to the table. I don't necessarily mean "book smart"—I mean a salesman who knows that customers—and the markets they're in—are dynamic. Consequently, client needs change over time, often quickly. A good closer knows this and is never surprised by market shifts. On the contrary, he or she anticipates them and is ready for the client's new needs before the customer even knows it.

Great closers are like Velcro. You never know when a client is (especially these days) ready to buy—especially these days when the economy has sales decisions taking longer than I can remember. Good closers have perfected the art of staying close to their clients without being overbearing about it. Customers appreciate that and reward Velcro closers with orders.

Great sales closers are partners. I've seen closers who routinely refer to their clients not as "they" but as "we"—like they were both in the trenches together. That's a great trait for a closer. When you treat your clients as partners, with all that entails (like honesty, patience, and understanding of the client's situation), you foster a mindset where the client knows you'll go into battle with them—no matter what.

Great closers have great timing. Sales professionals want to push for every sale they can get. But that isn't always wise. I've seen plenty of sales that were ill-advised and that should never have gone down. A good closer walks away from those deals when it becomes obvious that the sale will hurt more than help the client. That diplomacy wears well on customers, who will trust that salesman more deeply down the road.

In addition, the best sellers never sell for the sake of a commission—they believe in their product and/or service, and they know that it will solve their customers' problems.

Great closers also are confident closers. They honestly expect their customers to buy from them—they really expect to succeed. They keep the close simple and straightforward. The best closers know that the client has to be comfortable, so they make the close at the right pace, and with the client's comfort always a priority.

Q-Tip: *Planting Seeds, Harvesting Sales*

I'm an absolute animal about closing sales. It's the payoff from all that hard work—planting seeds, nurturing relationships, building trust, and then harvesting those sales relationships at exactly the right time.

When you think about it, creating and closing sales really is a lot like tending a garden. The seeds, the cultivation, the watering and tending, and finally, the harvest—it's amazing how symmetrical sales and gardening can be.

Take the key sales traits I've used over the years to build relationships and close sales. See how key sales steps equal key gardening steps:

Targeting clients = Planting seeds

Building rapport and trust = Nurturing and cultivating your plants

Getting your prospect's attention = talking (and listening) to your clients

Probing for problems, opportunities, needs, and values = Ridding your garden of pests and bugs, and dealing with bad weather

Demonstrating products based on the specific needs you have discovered = Trying out new tools and growth strategies to maximize your harvest

Asking for the business = Praying for a bountiful harvest

Closing the sale = Harvesting your crops

Get Out There and Sell

Ray Kroc, founder of McDonalds, had a great saying: "Be in business for yourself, but not by yourself."

That's how he described his business philosophy to his army of McDonald's franchisees. It's a great way to describe how sales professionals should act.

There's a term for that behavior. As defined, "intrapreneurship" is the act of behaving like an entrepreneur, except within a larger organization. That's exactly how successful salespeople should operate.

In order to jump-start your Sales Monster campaign, you must act like you own your own company. Most business owners operate under the mantra that "it's impossible to fail." I know I do.

If you can take that attitude into the sales trenches, you'll close more sales than you ever dreamed possible.

Now, it's time to get excited.

Do This	Not That
Do . . . take initiative, and go the extra step for clients.	*Don't . . . assume that your clients will be there for you forever—take no client for granted.*
Do . . . close like a master by focusing on your product and service—and how it solves your customer's problem.	*Don't . . . crowd your customer too close— practice pace and timing.*
Do . . . use the Monster Profile List included in this chapter. It will help you increase sales.	*Don't . . . ignore how regular customers can link you to future sales.*

Chapter Summary

- Be there for your customers—more than you thought possible.

- Build support and trust.

- Always ask for the business.

JUMP START NOW:

How High Can You Jump?

Let's end the book the same way I wrote it—with purpose and with a twist.

I'm going to begin the end with an anecdote about fleas.

That's right—fleas. I think the story encompasses a lot of what I've said in this book, especially about inspiring yourself to aim higher, and to reach goals you once thought impossible.

So how do fleas fit into out story? Hear me out.

Over the years, flea trainers have observed a predictable and strange habit of fleas while training them. Fleas are trained by putting them in a cardboard box with a top on it. The fleas will jump up and hit the top of the cardboard box over and over and over again. As you watch them jump and hit the lid, something very interesting becomes obvious. The fleas continue to jump, but they are no longer jumping high enough to hit the top. Apparently, sharp headaches force them to limit the height of their jumps.

When you take off the lid, the fleas continue to jump, but they will not jump out of the box. They won't jump out because they can't jump out. Why? The reason is simple. They have conditioned themselves to jump just so high. Once they have conditioned themselves to jump just so high, that's all they can do!

Many times, people do the same thing. They restrict themselves and never reach their potential. Just like the fleas, they fail to jump higher, thinking they are doing all they can do.

That's the challenge for sales professionals who feel like they have jumped as high as they can, and just can't jump higher anymore—if at all.

But as the book you hold in your hands or on screen has demonstrated, we all have a sales monster inside of us who wants more than anything else in the world to jump out of that box. That sales monster—who lives inside each one of us—is itching for a chance at reigniting that passion you once had for sales.

Believe me, it's there. And I think this book has shown that *you* know the passion is there.

So let's make sure you leave this book with that candle lit—with the passion and energy you need to awaken that sales monster inside of you.

To trigger that process, I've assembled the best fifty tips for igniting that passion for sales, and I'm including them all in this chapter. I figure it's the best way to send you back out into the sales arena, armed and ready with our seven "jump-start" steps to re-engaging that sales monster inside of you, as well as fifty action-oriented tips to help you make your sales-career goals and dreams a reality.

Remember, keeping that pilot light on all the time isn't a luxury in the sales game—it's a necessity. Keep that flame burning bright with these fifty tips, and we'll see you in the winner's circle in no time at all.

1. Don't be afraid to climb back into the ring. If you feel tired and stale, even fearful about reclaiming your sales mojo, know that failure isn't an option. Recall the lion tamer back in Chapter One who climbed back into the lion's den only nine days after being mauled. That takes guts—and it's a character trait that's in all of us.

2. Embrace failure—to a point. History is full of success stories of people who tripped on banana peels first. Remember that Walt Disney was once fired because he couldn't draw, and Henry Ford was ridiculed as a lousy car-maker. Look how they turned out.

3. Once you've failed, learn from it—and move on. It's highly useful to chalk up our slipups to experience, as long as we get a good lesson from the experience. But after that, let it go—it's a burden you don't want or need to carry.

4. Don't point fingers. In the end, sales success is all about the man—or woman—in the mirror. In other words—you. So don't waste time pointing fingers and assigning blame, even if you have a good case for it. Your success is defined by how hard you work and what you accomplish. In my book, optimists are accountable for their failures and their successes.

5. Take stock/reassess your career. The Chinese say a single journey starts with a single step. That first step should be a thorough assessment of your career; where you've been, where you've struggled, and where you have succeeded. With that knowledge, planning where you need to go to awaken the sales monster inside of you is that much easier.

6. Don't go it alone. Make sure you establish a network of friends, families, and coworkers to help you re-establish your career mojo. You can try, and I have, but it's hard to turn your sales career around by yourself. But with the strength of ten—the sky's the limit.

7. Set a crystal clear vision. This one is a personal favorite of mine—because I've tried it myself and it really works. Set your direction by setting a vision. The direction-setting aspect of taking charge of your sales career does not produce plans; it creates vision and strategies.

8. Look around you. What are the successful salespeople doing? How are the best sales producers getting the job done? What are the worst sales professionals doing wrong? Make sure to read books (I'm a big reader), attend good seminars, and check out the best sales stories online. They may have useful stories to tell.

9. See yourself as others see you. Ask around. Have your peers noticed a change in you? How are you perceived by clients, by your employers, by your fellow sales professionals? This one isn't easy—but it is necessary. Ask the tough questions and you'll get the best answers.

10. Take risks, but smart risks. Seize opportunities by taking risks—but make sure you have the facts, you know what the pros and cons are, and that your employer is in the loop.

Q-TIP: *Imagine the Impossible—Then Achieve It*

Every great achievement was once impossible until someone set a goal to make it a reality.

Lewis Carroll's famous masterpiece *Through the Looking Glass* contains a story that exemplifies the need to dream the impossible dream. There is a conversation between Alice and the queen, which goes like this:

"I can't believe that!" said Alice.

"Can't you?" the queen said in a pitying tone. "Try again, draw a long breath, and shut your eyes."

Alice laughed. "There's no use trying," she said. "One can't believe impossible things."

"I dare say you haven't had much practice," said the queen. "When I was your age, I always did it for half an hour a day. Why, sometimes I've believed as many as six impossible things before breakfast."

When you dare to dream, many marvels can be accomplished. The trouble is, most people never start dreaming their impossible dream.

---

11. Take a negative and turn it into a positive. We're all going to strike out once in a while, but we have to keep swinging. Babe Ruth knew that. He practiced "attitude control"—also known as the formidable power of affirmation. When something negative happens, find something positive to take from it. Then start swinging again.

12. Refuse to lose. This is the second half of the last tip. Like I said, we're all going to have setbacks. The key is to learn from them, and to put those experiences behind you as fast as possible. In short, stop looking backward and look forward.

13. Overcome adversity. Focus on leaping over obstacles. Find inspiration in Beethoven, who composed his most brilliant symphonies after he turned deaf.

14. Know that success isn't all that complicated. People tend to overthink what it takes to achieve in sales—and in life. Success is simple: assess your options, analyze them, and act on those options. One more thing—be happy while you do it.

15. Don't set huge, mind-boggling goals—set small, incremental ones. I'm going to leave this one alone—just think about it. As the old saying goes; "yard by yard, life is hard; but inch by inch, life's a cinch."

16. Listen. Let your clients do all the talking. Practice letting the other person talk, and focus on what he or she is saying. Your ears will make you more money than your mouth ever will.

17. Visualize the changes you want to make in your sales career. Try to articulate what you're trying to achieve in your transformation to a sales dominator. What do *you* want to be?

18. Get a mentor. When you're changing your life, it's highly useful to have someone who has your back. That's where a mentor can help. Find someone you can bounce ideas off of, soak information from, and commiserate with. Preferably, find someone who succeeded in sales and can help you do the same.

19. Find out what motivates you. Motivation is the oil that makes your sales engine purr like a Ferrari. What motivates you? Money? Adrenaline? The thrill of the chase? All three? Great! Channel them and ride the wave each generates. Don't fight against the wave—ride it as long as possible.

20. Plant seeds. When you plant good, fruitful seeds and you nurture them carefully, your harvest will be a bountiful one. Good seeding breeds opportunities, and good opportunities breeds sales. Plus, planting seeds is a great stress reducer.

Q-TIP: *Making a Negative a Positive*

Years ago in Scotland, the Clark family had a dream. Clark and his wife worked and saved, making plans for their nine children and themselves to travel to the United States. It had taken years, but they had finally saved enough money and had gotten passports and reservations for the whole family on a new liner to the United States.

The entire family was filled with anticipation and excitement about their new life. However, seven days before their departure, the youngest son was bitten by a dog. The doctor sewed up the boy but hung a yellow sheet on the Clarks' front door. Because of the possibility of rabies, they were being quarantined for fourteen days.

The family's dreams were dashed. They would not be able to make the trip to America as they had planned. The father, filled with disappointment and anger, stomped to the dock to watch the ship leave—without the Clark family. The father shed tears of disappointment and cursed both his son and God for their misfortune.

Five days later, the tragic news spread throughout Scotland—the mighty Titanic had sunk. The unsinkable ship had sunk, taking hundreds of lives with it. The Clark family was to have been on that ship, but because the son had been bitten by a dog, they were left behind in Scotland.

When Mr. Clark heard the news, he hugged his son and thanked him for saving the family. He thanked God for saving their lives and turning what he had felt was a tragedy into a blessing.

---

21. Be curious. I haven't met a good sales producer yet who wasn't inquisitive and who didn't want to learn about his or her business. As I said earlier in the book, if you're not curious and if you have no interest in learning something new, then you're not really trying. And you're also probably not cut out for a career in sales.

22. Learn from your customers. In sales, learning is earning. And the best source of knowledge isn't really in a book (as much as I love them). It's from your customers. Listening and learning from your customers is a direct route to closed sales. Lots of closed sales.

23. Ask good questions of your customers. You can't listen to your client forever—sooner or later you're going to have to state your case. Before you do, ask good questions. Start with these knowledge gainers:

- Who are you doing business with right now—and why?

- If they are your customers, ask what you're doing right—and wrong.

- Also, ask how you can improve.

- How does your knowledge source prefer to be sold to?

- What's the most effective mode of communication for your knowledge source?

24. When meeting a client, always learn at least one thing. Meetings with clients and potential clients are a golden opportunity to cement relationships and make sales. But under the radar, make sure each meeting has one goal—learn at least one thing you didn't know. Any nugget of new information can lead to a sale. So accumulating these nuggets is a good thing.

25. Don't focus on your product or service, focus on the customer. In sales, a big mistake we've all made is to make the product a priority, and we leave the client in the background. That's why it's critical that you make learning all you can about your customer your number one priority.

26. Know that sales is a two-way street. Whether you know it or not, a sale is being made every time you're working on a client. Either you're selling to the client or the client is selling to you. How? He or she is telling you why you're pitch is being rejected. Listen for the sale on the other side of the desk or phone and have an answer for "no."

27. Absorb and forget. When you're reading up on your customer, or on some good sales techniques, always make notes and highlight key passages. They tend to stick longer with you when you make an effort to note the good stuff (and you'll also forget the bad stuff).

28. My definition of a brand. Making people comfortable doing business with you. Better yet, making people want to do business with you.

29. Brand yourself. Branding is also who you are in the minds of your customers. Too many salespeople focus only on closing sales. They go through all the customary steps to close the deal, but never seek to separate themselves from the competitive pack.

30. What do you bring to the table? Create a personal brand that emphasizes your best qualities—dependability, persuasion, a sense of humor, and (especially) trust can be real brand-building cornerstones.

Q-TIP: *Not-So-Tiny Bubbles*

In 1879, Procter and Gamble's bestseller was candles. But the company was in trouble. Thomas Edison had invented the light bulb, and it looked as if candles would become obsolete. Their fears became reality when the market for candles plummeted since they were now sold only for special occasions.

The outlook appeared to be bleak for Procter and Gamble. However, at this time, it seemed that destiny played a dramatic part in pulling the struggling company from the clutches of bankruptcy. A forgetful employee at a small factory in Cincinnati forgot to turn off his machine when he went to lunch. The result? A frothing mass of lather filled with air bubbles. He almost threw the stuff away but instead decided to make it into soap. The soap floated. Thus, Ivory soap was born and became the mainstay of the Procter and Gamble Company.

Why was soap that floats such a hot item at that time? In Cincinnati, during that period, some people bathed in the Ohio River. Floating soap would never sink and consequently never got lost. So Ivory soap became a bestseller in Ohio and eventually across the country.

Like Procter and Gamble, never give up when things go wrong or when seemingly insurmountable problems arise. Creativity put to work can change a problem and turn it into a gold mine.

---

31. Good salespeople are like good poker players. They take risks, but well-designed ones that are set to trigger when opportunities arise.

32. Always tilt the playing field in your favor. You can't predict the future. Sales, like poker, gives you enough analysis and data so the probabilities of success are high when you decide to strike.

33. It takes confidence to take risks. In sales, you're always in the confidence business. Lose sight of that and you're in danger of losing confidence in yourself.

34. Get out of your comfort zone. Don't stay with the tried and true—that's how you lost your sales mojo in the first place. If you don't take risks, you don't get the rewards.

35. Taking risks doesn't mean making reckless moves. There's a big difference between smart, calculated risk, and wild, reckless risk. Smart risk is measured by listening, watching, and acting when others aren't as prepared as you are.

36. To get out of your comfort zone, create your own experience. You'll need to practice to really get out of your comfort zone. But if you practice making cold calls or persuading decision makers that you haven't approached before, you're creating your own experiences—and getting out of your comfort zone in the process.

37. Get professional help. No, not a therapist or anything like that. Just a trusted peer you can run ideas by, and talk about problems.

Enough said.

38. Manage risk by spreading it around. 100 percent of the weight doesn't have to fall on your shoulders. Spread the risk around and you won't be left holding the bag if things don't work out.

39. Take action. Do something every day to increase your chances of getting sales. Whether it's making one more phone call or writing one more thank you letter—do one more thing every day.

40. The "Fifteen-Minute Rule." Set aside fifteen minutes a day to cold-call, and train yourself in an area where you need help (with me, it's focusing on specifics). Don't let anyone interrupt you—it's your quality "sales monster" time.

Q-TIP: *The Ten-Cent Plan*

When young F. W. Woolworth was a store clerk, he tried to convince his boss to have a ten-cent sale to reduce inventory. The boss agreed, and the idea was a resounding success.

This inspired Woolworth to open his own store and price items at a nickel and a dime. He needed capital for such a venture, so he asked his boss to supply the capital for part interest in the store. His boss turned him down flat. "The idea is too risky," he told

Woolworth. "There are not enough items to sell for five and ten cents." Woolworth went ahead without his boss's backing, and not only was he successful in his first store, but eventually he owned a chain of F. W. Woolworth stores across the nation.

Later, his former boss was heard to remark, "As far as I can figure out, every word I used to turn Woolworth down cost me about a million dollars."

---

41. Try something different. To increase your chances of reaching a sales lead, call before or after work hours. Prospects are more relaxed when the workday is done, and are more likely to talk business with you. Use this opportunity to practice your "listening" skills.

42. Look right in front of you. Tap into existing customers for some great knowledge on what *all* customers might want. Ask them how they like to be sold, and what they expect from their sales contacts.

43. Go all www crazy. Get your company to fund your own "webinar" on a key industry topic—something that will cement your reputation as an expert in the field. People buy from experts, and webinars can help you get to that level.

44. Google them. Always Google the name of a new contact. Absorb all the information you can on the client, such as colleges and associations—things like that. Then bring those pieces of data up in a positive way when you meet. It will leave a good impression on your customer.

45. Always be selling. Industry statistics say that 65 percent of a salesperson's time is NOT selling. Turn that statistic on its head by selling constantly.

46. Go the extra mile for your client. Do it enough and you'll have a client for life.

47. Think Ahead. Be prepared for objections—especially when you're just about to close. The mark of a great closer is one who anticipates bad news, and is ready to act immediately on a client's behalf when it arrives on the scene.

48. Tech is great, but. Don't rely too much on technology to close sales. Getting in front of a client is still the best way to make your case and to influence buying behavior. Cell phones are great, but don't live or die by them.

49. Plan, Plan, and Plan. Jump-start sales by being consistent and having a purpose for every call or visit to a client. Planning your visits ahead of time is a great way to maximize any meeting's impact with a client.

50. GET EXCITED! You're a Sales Monster now—go out and act like one—and start closing more sales!

So it's over, you made it to the end of my little bit of sales wisdom. Now what? Well, let me leave you with the famous words from legendary football coach Dick Vermeil:

If you don't invest very much, then losing doesn't hurt very much and winning is not very exciting.

Now is the time to get recommitted to the greatest profession in the world—Sales! To go all in, to make that 100-percent investment in believing in yourself. Forget about what happened yesterday, last week, or last year. Look at today as the start. A new beginning. Remember how hard you worked at your first job, in your first relationship, or on your first home. That's the enthusiasm that will propel you forward.

Winners expect to win, every time. Find success in small achievements that will lead you to success with your larger goals.

Treat this book as a workbook, use it as your guide to more sales. Focus your energies, stay committed. Brand yourself the way you want others to see you. Always crave knowledge and information. Never stop learning. Do that little bit extra today and everyday. The results will come.

Remember the Golden Rule of Sales: Never Refuse A Breath Mint!

Lastly, thank you very much for your time.

www.ingramcontent.com/pod-product-compliance
Lightning Source LLC
Chambersburg PA
CBHW051315170526
45166CB00002B/555